Repairing and Reviving Furniture

New Illustrated Library of Home Improvement Volume 6

Repairing and Reviving Furniture

Prentice-Hall/Reston Editorial Staff

Prentice-Hall of Canada, Ltd. / Reston Publishing Company
Scarborough, Ontario

Series contributors/ H. Fred Dale, Richard Demske, George R.
Drake, Byron W. Maguire, L. Donald Meyers, Gershon
Wheeler

Design/Peter Maher & Associates
Color photographs/Peter Paterson/Photo Design

Printed and bound in Canada.

Contents

Chapter 1   Before You Begin   11

1-1.   The Critical Difference   11
1-2.   Do It Yourself?   13
1-3.   Looking for a Victim   13
1-4.   When an Antique Isn't an Antique   14

Chapter 2   Knowing Woods   15

2-1.   General Classifications   15
2-2.   Tree Structure   16
2-3.   Tree into Lumber   17
2-4.   Furniture Woods   18
2-5.   Plywood   18
2-6.   How Plywood Is Made   20
2-7.   Types of Hardwood Plywood   22
2-8.   Grades of Plywood   22
2-9.   Size and Thickness of Plywood   23
2-10.   History of Veneering   24
2-11.   Hardboard   24
2-12.   Common Furniture Woods   25

Chapter 3   Tools and Materials   29

3-1.   Buy Good Tools   29
3-2.   Essential Tools and Materials   29
3-3.   Optional Tools and Materials   39

3-4.   Specialty Tools and Materials 43
        a. *Upholstery* 44
        b. *Cane, Rush, Splints* 44
        c. *Painted and Decorative Finishes* 44
3-5.   The Importance of Adhesives 46
3-6.   Effect of Product Construction 47
3-7.   Wood Species 47
3-8.   Surface Protection or Finish 47
3-9.   Characteristics of Glue 49
3-10.   How Important Is Cost? 49
3-11.   Glues of Natural Origin 49
3-12.   Synthetic Resin Glues 50
3-13.   The Place Where You Work 52
3-14.   Workbench 52
3-15.   Work Platform 52

Chapter 4   Furniture Styles and Their History 55

4-1.   The Fickleness of Style 55
4-2.   The Older Styles 55
4-3.   Late Renaissance Elaborations 58
4-4.   Traditional and Provincial 58
4-5.   Early English 58
4-6.   Traditional English 60
4-7.   Later English 60
4-8.   Early French 61
4-9.   French Provincial 64
4-10.   American Colonial 64
4-11.   Italian Provincial 68
4-12.   Biedermeier 68
4-13.   Other Styles 68
4-14.   How to Recognize Styles 71

Chapter 5   Rudiments of Construction and Structural Repair 72

5-1.   Basic Construction 72
5-2.   Joinery 72
5-3.   Doing It Yourself 78
5-4.   Before You Start 78
5-5.   Taking Things Apart 78
5-6.   The Right Glue 80

5-7.   Preparation for Gluing 80
5-8.   Pressure 82
5-9.   Tourniquets 82
5-10.   Clamps 82
5-11.   Specific Jobs 91
         a. Loose Chairs (Lower Section) 91
         b. Loose Chair Parts 98
         c. Broken Arms and Legs 98
         d. Missing Parts 99
         e. Sticky Drawers 102
         f. Splits in Large Flat Parts 102
         g. Warps 102
         h. Loose Screws 104
         i. Working with Dowels 104
         j. Patches 104

Chapter 6   Cosmetic Repairs—Restoring and Reviving 106

6-1.   Cleaners and Conditioners 106
6-2.   Types of Finishes You'll Find 106
6-3.   Testing for Finishes 109
6-4.   Removing Wax 110
6-5.   White Spots and Rings 113
6-6.   Scratches, Gouges and Other Wounds—
         Wax Sticks 113
6-7.   Deep Wounds—Stick Shellac 115
6-8.   Cigarette Burns 115
6-9.   Dents and Bruises 115
6-10.   Cloudiness, Haziness, Blushing 116
6-11.   Cracking, Crazing, Alligatoring 116
6-12.   Reamalgamation Technique 118
6-13.   Cracked, Chipped Varnish 118
6-14.   Black Rings or Spots 119
6-15.   Scuffed Finishes 120
6-16.   Grease Spots 120
6-17.   Chipped or Peeling Paint 120
6-18.   Milk Paint 120
6-19.   Repairing Veneer and Inlays 121
6-20.   Patches 121
6-21.   Hardware Restoration 124
6-22.   Plastic 125
6-23.   Leather 125
6-24.   Marble Tops 125

Before You Begin

A common complaint these days is that everything costs more and wears out faster than it used to. One happy exception to at least the second part of this virtual rule is furniture. Given proper care, good furniture, as it always has, will last practically forever. "Proper care" means maintenance methods such as periodic waxing, polishing, and regluing of loose joints. But even when these jobs *are* done properly (which is rare), the best piece of furniture reaches a point where cosmetics can no longer hide its fatigue. Furniture, after all, is not designed primarily as art. It is mostly meant for seating, dining and storage.

It is at this crucial point, when the once proud possession gets a little creaky in the joints or wrinkled in its finish, that furniture often gets tossed aside for something younger and sturdier.

Fortunately for furniture, if not for *homo sapiens*, a complete rejuvenation is possible. The knowledgeable restorer is a veritable fountain of youth, able to do to wood what medical science and medieval explorers have failed to do for mankind.

The restorer takes a discarded piece of "junk", which he acquired for little or nothing, and turns it into a useful and decorative piece of furniture. If he is skilled at buying and restoring, he may even have a truly valuable antique which is worth many times the expense and effort it took him to restore it.

1-1. The Critical Difference

When is a piece worth saving — or buying — and when is it not worth the effort of restoration? At one level, it is true that anything is worth saving. We become attached to certain things in our lives, and an old chair or desk can acquire a sentimental value far beyond its real worth. Another coat of paint can keep "Grandpa's chair" in the family for a few more years. Also, the restoration of the old dining room set means that you don't have to buy a new one for three or four times more than you paid when you were first married.

If your goal, however, is more than sentiment or saving money (nothing wrong with either of those motives), there are certain criteria used by professional restorers which are useful in making a decision about whether to scrape or scrap. The same guidelines are generally true as well when deciding whether to buy an "antique" with restoration in mind.

Is a piece of genuine use to you? Even though it may be pretty, valuable, or a family heirloom, if you haven't got a place for it, get rid of it. There are some styles of furniture that just don't mix. Many old pieces are just too heavy and ponderous for modern décors. Maybe there isn't room for it.

What kind of shape is it in? Is it sturdy?

Fig. 1-1. By knowing how to repair and revive furniture, you can convert an old piece into something attractive and functional.

Loose joints can usually be fixed, but if it's poorly designed, can't hold its weight, is too spindly or coarse, maybe it isn't worth restoring. Look for signs of quality like dovetailed joints and easily opened drawers. Are there missing parts which can't be replaced easily? How much work will it take to get it into shape again? Maybe it just needs cleaning.

What is it made of? What kind of wood is used? (See Chapter 2.) If it's burl walnut, rosewood, or any of the other valuable woods, you should certainly not throw the piece out, no matter how ugly. Turn it into something else or shorten it. Take it to a professional cabinetmaker and have him do it for you; or even sell it. But don't throw out valuable woods (not that wood has the same value as an old coin or a painting, but some woods have a priceless beauty which shouldn't be wasted).

Perhaps the most important question in deciding whether or not to restore a piece of furniture is whether or not you like it; or, better, can you live with it? You may see something at an auction, in an antique shop or a flea market that looks like it might be a "valuable antique once it's fixed up". And well it might, but it's not worth a penny to you if you don't like it. Even when it's restored to its former beauty, you may hate it. It may clash horribly with the rest of your things. Sure, you can sell it (maybe) for more than you paid for it (maybe), but that isn't much of a reason to do all the work you're going to do to restore it.

Ultimately, the answers to the above questions will come after you have gained some experience. It's like finding a job — the employer wants someone with experience, and the only way you can get experience is by working. You can, however, keep these questions in mind, and depend on trial and error.

1-2. Do It Yourself?

You don't need any special talents to be able to restore furniture. You do need a certain respect for hard work, a little know-how and a "feel" for what will work. You can acquire all these things. What you cannot learn is perhaps the most vital factor of all — a real affection for and appreciation of good furniture. In particular, you need a deep respect for the craftsmanship and talent that produced the piece in the first place.

If you didn't want to do at least some restoration yourself, you wouldn't be reading this book. There are times, however, when you should turn the job over to the professionals. One of these times is when you stumble across what is truly a valuable antique. How to tell if something is valuable or not is another question, but if you have good reason to think that a piece is rare and old, take it to a reputable antique dealer for an appraisal. (He may charge you, but it'll be worth it.) In all probability the piece isn't worth as much as you thought it was. If it does prove to be valuable, however, don't touch it at all unless you are well experienced, and even then it may be wiser to pay a pro to do the job.

Whom do you contact? If you know someone in the field, fine. If not, the yellow pages are the quickest way. For appraisals, look under "Antiques — Dealers" and search for one that advertises that he does that type of work. Professional restorers and refinishers can be found in two places, right after the antique dealers under "Antiques — Repairing and Restoring", or under "Furniture — Repairing and Refinishing". Not all of the listees are qualified to appraise furniture. A careful reading of the listings, plus a phone call or two, should turn up someone who can help you. That a piece isn't valuable doesn't mean that it isn't worth restoring. If it isn't a rare antique, but a nice-looking piece that would enhance the looks of your home, then this is a job for you.

Formidable though the job may look, it really isn't that bad. Remember that the beauty of old furniture lies in the rich patina of the wood that has mellowed over the years. It isn't necessary (or desirable) to scrape the wood down to a point where it looks like new, raw material. All you have to do is get rid of the old worn-out finish.

Upholstered furniture may require little or lots of work, depending on how complicated the job was originally: dining room chair seats are easy, ornate sofas can be brutal, and tufted work is impossible for an amateur. The rule of thumb in upholstery is "try it". You can't really wreck anything except the material. If the job looks easy, give it a whirl. If it's obviously a complex operation, you can do the refinishing and send it to an upholsterer for the rest. Before you buy an upholstered piece, look for the tag certifying that the object has been sanitized. (See Chapter 3 in Volume 16 for more on upholstery.)

Furniture repair is another of those "iffy" problems. Minor repairs are fairly easy. Loose rungs and arms can be glued. Missing parts are sometimes easily duplicated, usually not. In this instance, unlike upholstery projects, you *can* ruin the piece by improper repair. If you're at all unsure, consult the yellow pages under "Furniture Repair and Refinishing". (Repairs are covered in Chapters 5 and 6.)

Before you do any of the above, however, consider the possibility of reviving the old finish with primitive materials such as a cleaner-conditioner, or a little warm water and lots of elbow grease. Many dull finishes are startlingly transformed with polish alone (see Chapter 6 for various effective ways to remove scratches and stains).

1-3. Looking for a Victim

The obvious place to look for an unsuspecting chair or table to start working on is in an antique shop. Most of these shops contain a wide range of pieces, from very good to horrible, the latter revealed by their bargain price. If you're completely new to refinishing and are afraid of bungling your first job, it may be wise to choose a small inexpensive piece. If you're confident of succeeding, pick out something you can use when you finish it (assuming it turns out all right).

Antique shops are poor places for bargains, though. A good antique dealer knows his furniture and isn't going to part with anything decent at a discount price. If you have the time and stamina to devote to the art of acquisition, attend such homespun functions as "garage" sales, flea markets and auctions. Shop Goodwill, Salvation Army and St. Vincent de Paul stores. Better yet, search the recesses of your own attic and basement and those of friends and relatives. Even junkyards and town dumps have been known to contain treasures.

Unfortunately, even these tried-and-true sources are becoming more competitive. Antique dealers, wholesalers or "scouts" will be outbidding you at auctions, and the Salvation Army is taking a closer look at donations in order to discover hidden treasures.

1-4. When an Antique Isn't an Antique

If you have real confidence in your ability to tackle a restoration job, or if you've had some experience in the art and are ready for something big, it's time to go back to that antique shop. You will pay a premium for shopping there, but most antique dealers are reliable and knowledgeable. They'll be happy to sell or steer you to a piece which needs renovation. Even though you will pay more for expert advice, you'll be reasonably sure of

getting something decent, and not just a castoff.

If you're shopping in the no-man's land of auctions, flea markets and garage sales, you're taking some real chances of being skinned. You may well pick up a bargain, but more often than not it will be pure junk.

Remember that according to the customs department, antiques are those items officially made before 1830 or unofficially over one hundred years old. (They're duty free.) Some experts would say that "antique" can mean something as young as fifty years. If it's younger than that, it simply doesn't qualify, no matter how it looks.

In the sense of the word we are using, "antique" is defined in the *Random House Dictionary of the English Language* as "any work of art, piece of furniture, decorative object, or the like, created or produced in a former period, usually over 100 years ago". *Webster's New Collegiate Dictionary* says that it is "a piece of furniture, tableware, or the like, made at a much earlier period than the present".

Many of the same guidelines about whether or not a piece is worth restoring apply to buying antiques. No matter how old something is, it isn't worth very much if it is poorly constructed, unattractive or irreparable. It is possible, of course, for something to be an authentic antique and not fit in with your decorating scheme. But if you can't use it, there still isn't much point in finishing it — unless, of course, you want to make a profit.

For the novice refinisher, it is much more practical to restore a good, serviceable piece than to try and make money by buying and selling antiques. Once you get good enough (and fast enough) you might consider going into the business of buying, restoring and reselling, but learn the fundamentals on something more modest.

Knowing Woods

If you know furniture at all, you know that almost any material imaginable is used in modern design — from glass to metal to molded plastics of various composition.

When people talk about repair and refinishing, however, invariably their discussion concerns wood furniture. Wood lends itself easily to effective restoration, and it is virtually the only material furniture makers had until recently. It is our most versatile building material; it is easily cut, shaped, fitted and joined, and can be finished to a rich warmth that cannot be matched by any other product.

It is imperative for the novice restorer to know as much as possible about wood. The characteristics of wood, as shown in the chart in Section 2-12, are vital guideposts in knowing how to repair and refinish. Some woods are porous, some are dense; some are soft, some are hard; some are light, some are dark. All of these qualities are important in determining the type of finish and degree of workability.

2-1. General Classifications

The two general classifications of lumber are softwood and hardwood. Softwood comes

Fig. 2-1. Only the large portion of the trunk, the "bole", is used for lumber.

Fig. 2-2. Lumber being transported to a mill for processing.

from evergreen trees (conifers) such as pine, cedar, spruce and fir. These trees keep their needle-like foliage the year round, and also produce cones. Hardwood is cut from broad-leaved trees (deciduous) — ash, oak, walnut, birch and elm are common varieties. These trees lose their foliage in the winter.

Fundamentally, both types of woods are made up of the same substances. The difference is in the arrangement of these elements. The millions of tiny hollow cells in a tree are packed tightly together in a honeycomb formation. In hardwoods, the cell walls are thick, making the wood dense, heavy and strong. Softwoods have thin wall cells, making them lighter and more porous.

2-2. Tree Structure

A tree is a complex structure of roots, trunk,

Fig. 2-3. Cross section of a log, showing annual rings.

limbs and leaves. Only the larger portion of the trunk or "bole" is used for lumber. This portion is first crosscut into logs.

In most species, wood at the center of the trunk (heartwood) is darker than wood in the outer part (sapwood) (Figure 2-3) and varies from it slightly in physical properties. The relative proportion of heartwood to sapwood in a tree varies with species and environment. Sapwood normally can be seasoned more easily than heartwood, and though sapwood is more easily impregnated with wood preservatives, there is no difference in strength.

When tree growth is interrupted or slowed each year by cold weather or drought, the structure of the cells formed at the end and the beginning of the growing season is different enough to define sharply the annual layers or growth rings. In many species, each annual ring is divided more or less distinctly into two layers. The inner layer, the springwood, consists of cells having relatively large cavities and thin walls. The outer layer, the summerwood, is composed of smaller cells. The transition from springwood to summerwood may be abrupt or gradual, depending on the kind of wood and growing conditions at the time it was formed. In most species, springwood differs from summerwood in physical properties, being lighter in weight, softer and weaker. Species such as the maples, gums and poplars do not show much difference in the structure and properties of the wood formed early or later in the season.

The strength of wood depends on the species, growth rate, specific gravity and moisture content. Extremely slow growth produces a weak wood. Softwoods also are weakened by extremely rapid growth. Wood with low specific gravity or high moisture content is generally weak. Defects such as grain deviation caused by spiral growth, knots and burls also result in wood that is weaker than normal wood.

Yet these structural defects frequently enhance the appearance of wood. Spiral growth results in a winding stripe on turnings. Butt wood shows the assembly of root branches, and crotch wood has a merging or diverging pattern. A burl produces attractive boards showing tissue distortion. "Bird's-

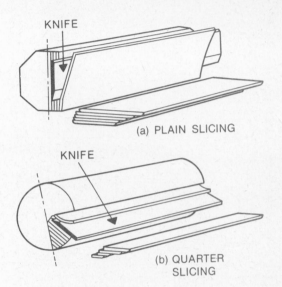

Fig. 2-4. Methods of sawing lumber.

eye" figures result from the elliptical arrangement of wood fibers around a series of central spots. Some quartersawed woods show pronounced whitish flakes where the wood rays are exposed. This forms an interesting pattern, especially in oak and sycamore.

2-3. Tree into Lumber

Lumber is sawed from a log in two different ways, with the plane of the cut either radial or tangential to the annual rings (Figure 2-4). When the cut is at a tangent to the annual rings, the lumber is called "plainsawed" (hardwoods) or flat-grain lumber (softwoods). When the cut is in a radial plane (parallel to the wood rays), the lumber is called "quartersawed" (hardwoods) or edge- or vertical-grain lumber (softwoods). Generally, lumber with annual rings at angles from 45° to 90° is considered quartersawed, while lumber with rings at angles from 0° to 45° with the surface is considered plainsawed.

The relative advantages of the two types of cuts are that plainsawed is usually cheaper because it can be cut from the log faster and with less waste. It is less likely to collapse from drying. Shakes and pitch pockets extend through fewer boards. Round or oval knots affect surface appearance and strength less than the spike knots in quartersawed boards. Figures formed by annual rings and other grain deviations are more conspicuous.

Quartersawed lumber shrinks and swells less in width than plainsawed lumber. It cups and twists less, does not surface-check or split as badly in seasoning and use. It also wears more evenly and raised grain caused by the annual rings is not as pronounced. Quartersawed wood is less pervious to liquids with most species holding paint better. Figures resulting from pronounced rays, interlocked grain and wavy grain are more conspicuous. Width of the sapwood appearing in a board is no greater than that of the sapwood ring in the log.

As it comes from the sawmill, lumber has a high moisture content and is unsuited for use in furniture (or anything else). It is important that lumber be seasoned until the moisture content is in equilibrium with the conditions under which the wood will be in service. When a condition of equilibrium moisture content is reached, the lumber has no tendency to shrink, expand or warp. Because of normal changes in atmospheric moisture, this condition never holds constant. It is desirable, however, that an approximate equilibrium moisture content be reached.

Lumber can be seasoned by natural air-drying, by kiln-drying, or by various chemicals (common salt, urea) in combination with the other methods. The time available for drying, the species of wood, and the ultimate use of the wood are important factors in determining the method of seasoning. Kiln-drying is the common commercial practice. Chemical seasoning in combination with air- or kiln-drying is used for seasoning some high-quality lumber.

2-4. Furniture Woods

Certain characteristics are particularly desir-able in wood used to make furniture. These include:

- stability, or ability to keep its shape without shrinking, swelling or warping

- ease of fabricating, surfacing and finishing

- pleasing appearance (which may actually include some surface defects in the lumber)

- suitable strength and grain characteristics

- availability.

Invariably, the best furniture is made of hardwoods, although some fine Colonial-style furniture has been constructed from white pine and other softwoods. Hardwoods contain all of the qualities listed above to a greater and lesser degree. Softwoods ordinarily lack the desired degree of stability, strength and grain characteristics. Furthermore, their appearance is suitable only for the specific "rustic" look of primitive furniture, such as Early American. Softwoods are perfectly acceptable for painted furniture, however.

2-5. Plywood

Most people think of plywood as the big 4' × 8' sheets used for homebuilding or do-it-yourself projects. These, indeed, are the primary uses for plywood made of softwoods. In furniture making, however, rather extensive use is made of hardwood plywood.

For some people, the highest mark of quality in furniture is that it is made of "solid" mahogany or "solid" oak. Actually, such solid wood is used only for legs, rungs, etc., and would be not only wasteful, but also less attractive than veneered hardwood (or plywood) for flat surfaces. Veneer takes advantage of the best methods of cutting the wood while retaining the strength that plywood has. An increasingly important virtue of the

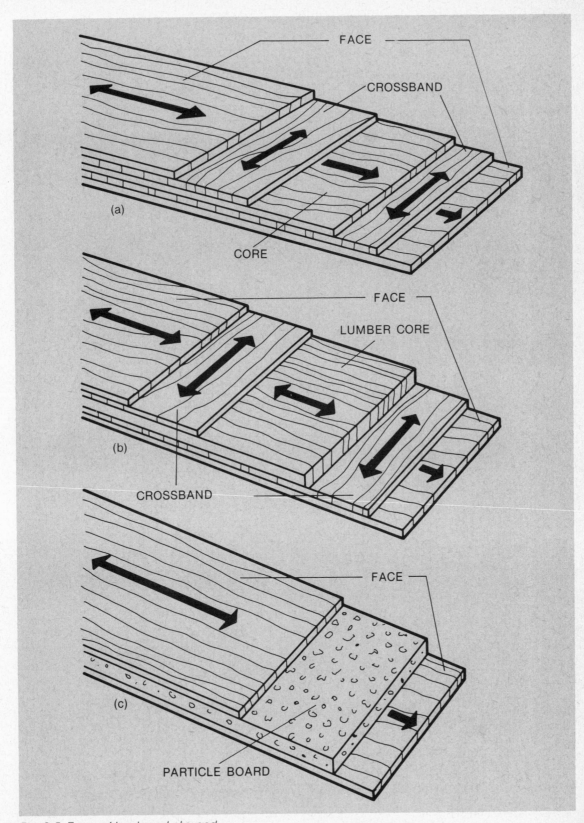

Fig. 2-5. Types of hardwood plywood.

veneering process is the efficient utilization of rare and valuable species of wood. Low-grade veneers can be used on the interior (and usually the back) without affecting the appearance of the final product.

Plywood is composed of thin plies of veneers that are glued together with the grains at right angles. Three-ply plywood has a center core faced with two veneers. Five-ply plywood has a core, two inner plies or "cross-bands", and a veneer facing. Plywood provides strength in both length and width, and has good resistance to splitting and moisture changes. (Certain plywood varieties are put together with waterproof glue and are suitable for exterior use.) Plywood can also be bent or formed.

The most common types of hardwood plywood are:

Veneer Core — all inner plies are of wood veneer, cut from a less expensive grade than the exterior plies.

Particleboard Core (Figure 2-5) — interior is made of chips or pieces of wood combined with an adhesive binder. Also referred to as chipboard or chipcore. Used for kitchen cabinetry and similar work.

Lumber Core (Figure 2-5) — center consists of strips of wood several inches wide, bonded together, with a layer of cheaper veneer on both sides of that and the back and face veneers outside of those.

There are many other combinations of wood veneers and other exotic materials such as hardboard, kraft paper, plastic foam and aluminum foil, but the best and most commonly used material for furniture is lumber-core hardwood plywood.

2-6. How Plywood Is Made

Hardwood logs can be cut in four different ways to produce plywood. Of these, the first three result in no sawdust, further increasing the efficient, maximum utilization of the cut logs.

Prior to use, most hardwood logs are heated to make cutting easier and to help insure smooth-cut veneer. The four methods used are the following:

Rotary Lathe (Figure 2-6) — the log is chucked in the center of each end and the log rotates against a knife, producing veneer, like unwinding a roll of paper. A bold, variegated grain pattern is generally evident in rotary cutting. Eighty percent to 90 percent of all veneer is cut by this method.

Slicing — most slicers consist of a stationary knife. The flitch, or section to be cut, is attached to a log bed which moves up and down; on each downward stroke a slice of veneer is cut by the knife. Slicers are used primarily for cutting decorative face veneers from woods such as walnut, mahogany, cherry and oak.

Stay-Log Cutting — this method makes veneers intermediate between rotary cut and sliced veneer. A rotary lathe is used; a flitch is attached to a "stay log" or metal beam, mounted in the lathe off-center. The stay-log method produces half-round veneer, which is generally used for faces.

Sawn Veneer — a very small quantity of veneer is cut in this manner. A type of circular saw called a "segment" saw, with a thin, interrupted blade, turns on an arbor. The thin blade reduces saw kerf. This method generally is used only for certain species and to achieve special effects. Oak and Spanish cedar are often cut by this process.

After rotary veneers are cut, they may go directly to a "clipper", which cuts the veneers into manageable rectangular sections, or they may be stored temporarily on a series of horizontal storage decks or on reels. From the clippers the veneers go to the dryers — large chambers equipped with heating elements and fans and having automatic conveying systems on which the veneer moves. Some mills now use high-speed dryers located behind the rotary lathe to dry the veneer in a continuous sheet after it is cut. Veneers are generally dried to moisture contents of below 10 percent — a level compatible with gluing and consistent with the moisture content that hardwood plywood products will be exposed to in service.

Fig. 2-6. Log being cut on a rotary lathe.

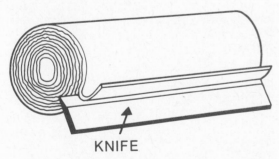

KNIFE

After drying, undersized sheets are dry-clipped and joined together to form full-size sheets. Taping machines and tapeless splicers are used in this joining process, which is followed by patching and repairing.

The veneers are now ready for gluing. Alternate ply veneers are fed through a glue spreader which coats both sides of the sheets with liquid glue. The spreader rollers control the amount of glue transferred to the veneer. Now comes the most important step in the process — the pressing together of the veneers. Heat (around 250° F.) and pressure (150 to 300 pounds per square inch) are applied by means of a hot press. Presses have as many as 35 or more openings, each capable of pressing one thick panel or two thin panels. After pressing, the panels are stacked for conditioning, sawed to dimension and sanded. They are then ready for inspection, grading, strapping, and shipping. Grading and inspection usually are done at intermediate steps in the manufacturing process.

2-7. Types of Hardwood Plywood

Interior hardwood plywood is designated as Type II plywood, and is the type most commonly used in furniture. It is made using urea resin adhesives and is water-resistant, but not waterproof. It should not be used outside.

Type I hardwood plywood is designed for outdoor use, with a glue bond consisting of phenol, resorcinol, phenolresorcinol, melamine or melamine-urea waterproof adhesives. There is also a Type III hardwood plywood, designed for containers and other rare usages, which has a urea resin base mixed with more water or extenders or both than Type II.

2-8. Grades of Plywood

Hardwood grading is complicated since more than one piece of wood may be used in each veneer, and the patterns and color are taken into consideration. The more important of the many grades are:

Premium Grade (A) – The face veneer may be made from more than one piece. With most species, multi-piece faces must be book matched, or slip matched (Figure 2-7). The quality of veneer is high – only a few small burls, occasional pin knots, slight color streaks, and inconspicuous small patches are allowed.

Good Grade (1) – The faces are similar to that of Premium Grade faces except that matching is not required. Sharp contrasts in color and great dissimilarity in grain and figure of two adjacent pieces of veneer in multi-piece are not allowed. This grade of veneer allows only a few small burls, occasional knots, slight color streaks, and inconspicuous small patches.

Sound Grade (2) – This grade provides a smooth surface. The veneer need not be matched for grain or color, but must be free of open defects.

Utility Grade (3) – Open defects are

(a) BOOK MATCHING

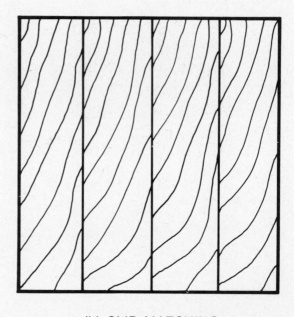

(b) SLIP MATCHING

Fig. 2-7. Book matching and slip matching of hardwood plywood.

allowed: knotholes up to one inch in diameter, wormholes and splits not exceeding 3/16″

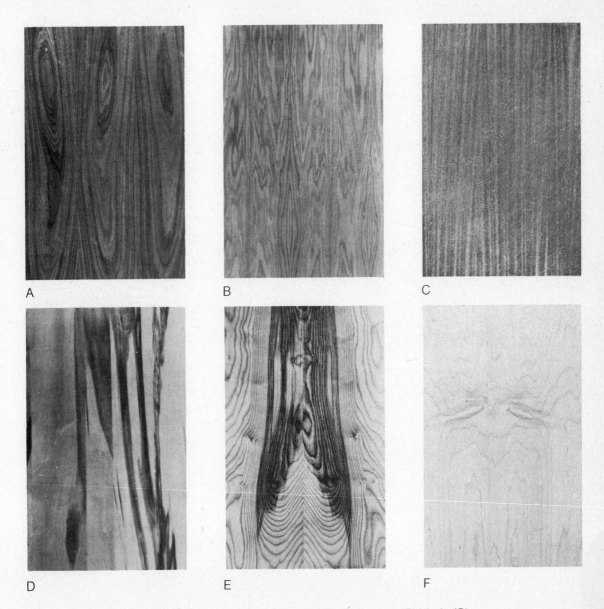

Fig. 2-8. Wood grains: (A) mahogany; (B) oak; (C) walnut; (D) maple; (E) birch; (F) gum.

wide and not extending half the length of the panel are permitted.

Backing Grade (4) – This grade is similar to Utility Grade except that larger-sized open defects are permitted: knotholes not greater than three inches, and splits up to 1″ wide, depending on the length of the split.

Plywood not conforming to any of the foregoing grades is called Specialty Grade, the characteristics of which must be agreed on by the buyer and seller.

2-9. Size and Thickness of Plywood

Hardwood plywood can be made in many sizes and thicknesses. Aircraft plywood and other specialty-use plywoods as thin as 3/64″ are not uncommon. One of the standard thicknesses for flush doors is 2-1/4″.

The size of the plywood panel depends

largely on its intended use. A standard panel is 4' wide and 8' long. A number of producers are capable of making plywood 5', 6' or 7' wide by 12' long. With special scarfing equipment, panels can be made as long as 40' or more, the maximum size depending largely on transportation and handling limitations.

2-10. History of Veneering

The art of veneering has been known for many centuries. One of the earliest records is a mural which archaeologists unearthed in Egypt and have dated at 1500 B.C. The mural shows workmen cutting veneer by means of a tool much like a hatchet; the glue pot over a fire suggests that adhesive used in that period was some type of animal glue. The thin sheets of veneer were spread with glue, and pressure was applied by sandbag weights. Artifacts of Egyptian furniture taken from sealed tombs in the past century show that the first plywood manufactured by man was used in overlaid and inlaid furniture.

One historian describes how the Greeks decorated with wood veneers. The Romans also were early users of veneer and plywood. Most historians believe that the primary use of plywood in these two cultures was to achieve beautiful decorative effects by the use of highly figured veneer. Articles of furniture overlaid with veneer in these times were highly treasured articles. There is little reference to the use of veneer in the years that followed until the seventeenth and eighteenth centuries when a revival of this art occurred in western Europe. In 1830, the piano industry became the first to use plywood. The earliest veneer-cutting lathe is described by Jon Dresser's American patent of 1840; however, it was not until some 35 years later that the veneer slicer was developed. The second half of the nineteenth century saw plywood being used to make chairs, desk tops, sewing machines, organs and other articles of furni-

Fig. 2-9. Applying veneer strip.

ture. The early years of the twentieth century brought the inception of the stock panel idea. A panel made in standard size (originally 3' × 6') could be cut into smaller sizes as desired.

2-11. Hardboard

Hardboard is not ordinarily a component of fine furniture, but it is used often for "snag-proof" drawer bottoms, case and mirror backs, and other uses where strength is more important than looks. (Specially finished hardboard panels, however, are in wide use for room panelling and may someday be perfected for use in better furniture.) Since you may encounter hardboard in your work, you should know what it is.

To make hardboard, logs are chipped down, and the chips are reduced mechanically into fiber bundles. These are then separated into individual fibers and formed into a mat, or thick, wet blanket of loose fibers. When compressed in giant hot presses, the result is a grainless, dense, uniform panel ready to be humidified and trimmed to size.

Hardboard, by definition, is more dense than wood and other composition panels, and is therefore stronger and more durable, better able to resist dents, abrasion, scuffing and hard use. It has excellent natural water resistance, but with tempering additives or other special processing it attains further improved moisture resistance, increased strength and extra durability. Because it has no grain, it is equally strong in all directions.

Like the wood from which it is made, hardboard is easily sawed, shaped, routed, drilled, bent and die-cut. It is free of slivers and splinters. Its smooth hard surface is an ideal base for most types of opaque finishes or decorative surfacing materials with no grain to raise or check the surface.

Hardboard is also used in cabinet building and can be shaped or molded into chair backs and seats. Perforated hardboard is often used for specialty purposes such as hanging tools or displaying items. Many people refer to hardboard as "Masonite", a manufacturer of hardboard.

2-12. Common Furniture Woods

Wood	Color of Heartwood	Color of Sapwood	Pattern Figure	Strength	Uses
Alder, red (Alnus rubra)	Light pinkish brown to white	Same	Obscure	Medium	Panel cores, table tops, sides, drawer fronts, exposed parts of kitchen furniture. Stains readily in imitation of mahogany or walnut.
Ash, green, black, white (Fraxinus)	Light grayish brown	White	Pronounced	High in bending	Solid tables, dressers, wardrobes.
Beech (Fagus grandifolia)	White to slightly reddish	Same	Obscure	High	Chairs and exterior parts of painted furniture. Bends easily and is well adapted for curved parts such as chair backs. Also used for sides, guides, and backs of drawers, and for other substantial interior parts.
Birch, yellow and black (Betula)	Light to dark reddish brown	White	Varying from a stripe to curly	High	Solid and veneered furniture. Same uses as hard maple.

Cherry, black (Prunus serotina)	Light to dark reddish brown	White	Obscure	Medium	Solid furniture. Relative scarcity causes it to be quite expensive.
Chestnut (Castanea dentata)	Grayish brown	White	Conspicuous	Medium	Cores of tables and dresser tops, drawer fronts, and other veneered panels. Used with oak in solid furniture.
Elm, American and rock (Ulmus)	Light grayish brown often tinted with red	White	Conspicuous	High	Used to some extent for exposed parts of high-grade upholstered furniture. Easily bent to curved shapes such as chair backs.
Gum, red (Liquidambar styraciflua)	Reddish brown	Pinkish white	Obscure to figured	Medium	Gum furniture may be stained to resemble walnut or mahogany. Also used in combination with these woods.
Gum, tupelo (Nyssa aquatica)	Pale brownish gray	White	Obscure to striped	Medium	Cores of veneered panels, interior parts, framework of upholstered articles.
Mahogany (Swietenia, Khaya)	Pale to deep reddish brown	White to light brown	Ribbon or striped	Medium	All solid and veneered high-grade furniture, boat construction, and cabinet work.
Maple, hard (Acer saccharum)	Light reddish brown	White	Obscure to figured	High	Bedroom, kitchen, dining, and living room solid furniture. Some veneer (highly figured) is used. Most furniture is given a natural finish.
Oak, red & white (Quercus)	Grayish brown	White	conspicuous	High	Solid and veneered furniture of all types. Quartered-oak furniture compares favorably with walnut and mahogany pieces.

Pine, ponderosa (Pinus ponderosa)	Light reddish	White	Obscure	Medium	Painted furniture.
Poplar, Yellow (Liriodendron tulipifera)	Light yellow to dark olive	White	Obscure	Medium	Cross banding of veneers, inexpensive painted furniture, interior portions of more expensive furniture, frames of upholstered articles.
Rosewood (Dalbergia nigra)	Dark reddish brown with black	White	Obscure, streaked	High	Piano cases, inlays, musical instruments, handles, etc.
Sycamore, (Platanus occidentalis)	Reddish brown	Pale reddish brown	Obscure to flake	High	Drawer sides, interior parts, framework of upholstered articles.
Tanquile (Shorea)	Pale to dark reddish brown	Pale grayish to reddish brown	Ribbon or stripe	Medium	Similar to mahogany.
Walnut black (Juglans nigra)	Light to dark chocolate brown	Pale brown	Varying from a strip to a wave	High	All types of solid and veneered furniture.

Selected Face Woods Categorized by Color:

Light Colored Woods: Ash, Birch, Cativo, Hackberry, Limba, Maple, Pine

Medium Colored Woods: Butternut, Cherry, Chestnut, Elm, Hickory, Lauan, Mahogany, Oak, Pecan, Persimmon, Sycamore, Teak

Dark Colored Woods: Ebony, Red Gum (heartwood), Paldao, Rosewood, Walnut

Selected Face Woods Listed by Specific Gravity:

Ebony	.90	Ash	.60	Sycamore	.49
Rosewood	.78	Maple (Hard)	.60	Limba	.48
Persimmon	.75	Walnut	.55	Mahogany	.47
Hickory	.72	Hackberry	.53	Chestnut	.43
Oak	.68	Red Gum	.52	Lauan	.43
Pecan	.66	Maple	.50	Cativo	.42
Teak	.66	Elm	.50	Pine (White)	.39
Paldao	.65	Cherry	.50	Butternut	.38
Birch	.62				

Cores for Hardwood Plywood Panels:

Core Type	Panel Thickness	Advantages	Disadvantages
Veneer (all inner plies of wood veneers)	1/4" (3 ply) or less	Inexpensive	Difficult to machine. Exposed edge shows core voids and imperfections. Most susceptible to warping (doors).
	5/16"-1/2" (5-ply)	Inexpensive	
	Over 1/2" (7-ply)	Best screw-holding power	
Particleboard	1/4" (infrequent) through 2" (usually 3 plies)	Most stable; least expensive (generally)	Poor edge screw-holding; heaviest core.
Lumber Core (consists of strips of lumber 1-1/2" to 4" wide)	5/8" thru 2" (usually 5 plies)	Easiest machined; exposed edges are solid; stable construction.	Most expensive, worst overall screw-holding.

Tools and Materials

Did you ever see a serious fisherman with a cheap reel? Or an experienced hunter with a bargain-store shotgun? Yet it is all too common for people to try something as time-consuming and delicate as furniture restoration with inadequate tools and materials. To save a dollar or less on a tool, they take the chance of negating hours of work spent on a restoration project.

3-1. Buy Good Tools

Furniture is expensive; so is your time. If you intend to work with both of these precious commodities, it is foolhardy to jeopardize them by using inferior equipment. This doesn't mean that you should throw away your money by buying every expensive tool you can find. It does mean that you should determine what tools you will need, and buy the best possible tool for the best bargain. It means not picking up cheap hammers and screwdrivers from bargain counters in supermarkets. It means spending some money for some power equipment, such as an orbital sander and 1/4-inch drill.

You don't have to buy everything at once, though. Take one project at a time, figure your needs for it, then buy what you need (and, if something happens to be on sale you'll need next time, pick that up too).

There are probably few people in this world who do not own some kind of hammer, a saw, a screwdriver or two and some sort of measuring device (if only a tape measure). In addition to these common household tools, there are several tools which are a must for any job, and a host of special ones which you may or may not want to buy. It all depends on the type of restoring you want to do. Do you, for example, want to get involved with seat caning, gold leaf, and all the many special finishing techniques used in painted furniture? You'll need special tools and materials. We will divide the tools and materials, then, into three categories: essential, optional and specialty.

3-2. Essential Tools and Materials

No matter what you're finishing, you'll need certain tools to repair the structure and prepare the finish.
Repairing

- Electric 1/4-inch or 3/8-inch drill with large set of bits. Works better than a bit and brace and costs less overall.

- Clamps — lots of them and in varying sizes. Get a pair of each kind you can find. Wood

Fig. 3-1. Electric 1/4-inch drill is an essential tool for repairing furniture.

or hand-screw clamps will be vital; C-clamps are the most versatile. For long stretches you'll need pipe or bar clamps. (See Section 5-10 for more on clamps.)

● Glue — lots of it and of different types. Glue is the major material for holding furniture together, with screws, nails or other devices used primarily to hold the wood together until the glue sets. Be sure to have some animal or fish glue, "white", plastic resin and casein glues around. (See Section 5-6.)

● Rope — nylon is the best, but almost any kind will do, even a piece of old clothesline. Rope is used in making tourniquets around legs and arms, often the only way to apply the proper type of pressure.

● Knife — a well-sharpened Boy Scout or "stockman's" knife is fine. Also have an old dull knife around for such jobs as scraping off old glue and cleaning out holes.

● Wooden mallet — a rubber, leather or soft plastic one can substitute.

● Dowels — in addition to glue, the best way to hold two pieces of wood together. They come in the form of sticks which you cut yourself, or sometimes you can buy a package of precut, different-sized dowels from a lumber or hardware store. Dowel sticks also make good rung replacements.

● Screws — not as good as glue for holding wood together, but sometimes the only way. Have some around, if only to hold the joint until the glue dries.

● Wood toothpicks and matches — these are handy for filling up loose joints (in conjunction with glue, of course).

● Razor blades (single edge) — not really an *essential* tool, but cheap enough so you can afford to invest in a few. Used for cutting veneers.

● Wood dough — often referred to by one of

Fig. 3-2. You'll need many types of clamps; these hand screws are useful.

Fig. 3-3. Wood dough may be used to plug counterbored screw holes.

its most popular brand names, "Plastic Wood". Used for filling in missing wood areas where surface appearance is not important. Strong, workable, can be cut, sawed, screwed and nailed into.

- Angle irons, braces — purists will tell you not to use these metal braces, and they shouldn't be used unless all other forms of bracing have been exhausted. Useful, though, when all else fails.

- Backsaws — these are so named because of a reinforcing rib along the back. They come in various sizes, but there is no need to get all of them at once. Start with the largest one, about 12 teeth to the inch (miter box saw). Others range up to 20 teeth per inch and are called dovetail saws, veneer saws and razor saws (largest to smallest). You can add these as you go along, if you wish.

- Sandpaper, files, rasps (assortment) — you'll need some of each for cutting wood down to size. Start small and add to your collection as you go along. Don't skimp on the sandpaper, though. It's not expensive. (See accompanying chart for sizes and types of abrasive paper.)

- Smoothing plane — the basic plane, essential for cutting large boards evenly, especially on the edges.

- Sanding block — preferably with a small pad. Makes sanding so much easier you'll wonder how anyone does without it. You can make a serviceable one of your own easily enough out of a piece of 2″ × 4″.

- Scratch awl — you wouldn't think you'd use it much, but once you've got it, you wonder how you managed without it. Useful for marking for saw cuts, starting screw holes, etc.

- Wood-marking gauge — a necessity for marking boards lengthwise. Scribes lines equidistant from the designated side.

Fig. 3-4. Use a smoothing plane to cut the edges of large boards.

- Nailset — not so much for driving nails as for knocking out dowels, plugs. You could buy a center punch, but you can also use the nailset for setting nails.

Lumberyard.

- General tools — those found already in most homes: crosscut saw, hammer, screwdriver, pliers, folding and steel rule, pencil.

Finishing

- Brushes, old — used, cheap paintbrushes for applying paint removers and other substances.

- Brushes, new — used for applying paint, varnish and shellac. Two-inch brushes are the best for non-specialized work.

- Brushes, artist — a few varying sizes for touchups and special effects.

- Putty knife — for applying wood dough, lifting off old paint and varnish after it has

been softened by removers, and assorted tasks. Use the oldest one, with rounded corners, for scraping.

- Scrapers — wide-bladed knives for large areas. If you haven't got an old one, file down the sharp corners for scraping.

- Toothbrushes, old — for scrubbing off old paint and varnish after a remover has been applied.

- Orange sticks (or meat skewers) — for digging into molding and crevices to remove old paint and varnish.

- Steel wool — buy in pads, starting with a mixed package from 1/0 to 3/0 grades, if available. Used for mopping up and cleaning off the messy residue left by paint and

Fig. 3-5. A two-inch brush is suitable for non-specialized work.

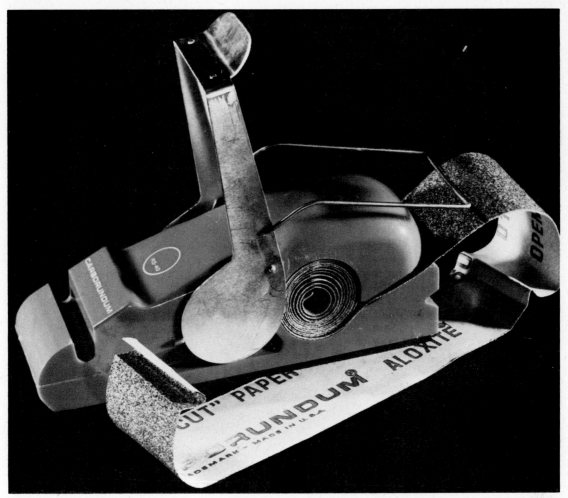

Fig. 3-6. A hand-held sander such as this ensures that you won't round off edges.

varnish removers, as well as for other fine abrasive jobs throughout the finishing process.

● Chemical paint removers — generally speaking, the jelly-like removers are the best for all-round use. (See Section 1-3, Volume 16 for details on selection and use.)

● Linseed oil — for various uses, including color restoration. Have at least one small can each of both raw and boiled oil.

● Denatured alcohol — many uses in reviving and removing old finishes, notably shellac.

● Rottenstone and pumice — two fine pow-

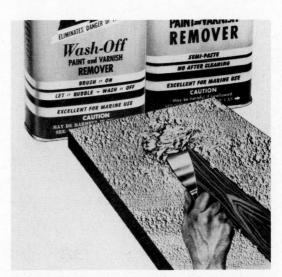

Fig. 3-7. Chemical paint and varnish removers are indispensable.

Tools used to repair furniture.

Corner cupboard and caned chair.

ders used in hand-rubbing finishes and reviving old ones. Rottenstone is a little finer than pumice. Use 3/F or 4/F pumice.

- Turpentine – used for reviving old finishes, as well as for paint cleaning and removing.

- Shellac sticks, wax sticks and a box of crayons – for filling in scratches and

gouges.

- Stains, fillers, bleaches, varnishes, shellac, paints and other finishing materials are obviously essential, but are not included here because of their wide variety. You will need some of them all of the time, and all of them some of the time (see Chapters 1 and 2 of Volume 16).

Selection Chart for Abrasive Paper

(Boldface indicates those most commonly used in furniture work)

Grit	Grade	Description	Use
20	3	Very coarse	Machine floor sanding,
24	3-1/2	Very coarse	Not used for furniture
30	2-1/2	Coarse	Not used for furniture
36	2	Coarse	Not used for furniture
40	1-1/2	Coarse	Not used for furniture
50	1	Medium	Occasionally used for rough wood and paint removal.
60	1/2	Medium	Occasionally used for rough wood and paint removal.
80	1/0	Medium	Paint removal and rough shaping
100	2/0	Fine	Preparatory softwood sanding
120	3/0	Fine	Preparatory hardwood sanding
150	4/0	Fine	Preparatory hardwood sanding
180	5/0	Fine	Preparatory hardwood sanding
220	6/0	Very Fine	Finish softwood sanding
240	7/0	Extra Fine	Finish hardwood sanding
280	8/0	Extra fine	Finish hardwood sanding
320	–	Superfine	Polishing finishes between coats, often used wet
360	9/0	Superfine	Polishing finishes between coats, often used wet
400	10/0	Superfine	Polishing finishes between coats, often used wet
500	–	Superfine	Used rarely for furniture work, mostly
600	–	Superfine	for plastics, ceramics, stone and metals, used wet

3-3. Optional Tools and Materials

These are the items which are nice to have around if you can afford them and can buy them one at a time. Some are just time-savers; others will be absolutely essential if and when you need them. It depends on the job at hand.

Repairing

● Bit and brace — for some, this drill offers more control than an electric drill. It also works better with the larger-sized augers. If you are used to one, continue using it. If not, the electric is really better.

● Center punch — useful when working with dowels or other items requiring exact centers. Essential for starting holes in metal.

● Dowel pins — grooved pins for use when inserting dowels in matching pieces, more for new or reconstructed work than for old work.

● Dowel jig — also useful when fabricating new pieces, as under "Dowel pins".

Fig. 3-9. A jointer, a drill press and a table saw are helpful if you can afford them.

● Drill press — useful for the kind of intricate work involved in dowel-making and joinery. (See Chapter 5 for a discussion of joinery.)

● Power sander — as you progress, you'll probably want both a straight-line and orbital sander. Start with the orbital. (Rotary sanders are not used on furniture.)

Fig. 3-8. A dowel jig is optional rather than essential for your workshop.

Fig. 3-10. The finishing sander gives wood surfaces a fine, smooth finish.

Fig. 3-11. A combination plane and rasp is useful on curved surfaces.

- Lathe – essential for forming new legs, etc. Get one of these only after you've mastered the basic steps described in this book.

- Planes, block and jack – for new work, mostly, but useful when forming new parts that have flat surfaces. The block is for small work; the jack for long, straight cuts.

- "Surform" plane – a combination plane and rasp that is useful on curved surfaces.

- Radial arm or table saw – for new work, mostly, but handy when you need one. Particularly good for joinery, multiple cuts, moldings or other fancy designs with special cutters.

- Handsaws – a large variety, depending on your need and budget. After the essential ones previously described, get a ripsaw, keyhole and coping saw. Then maybe a hacksaw, crosscut saw of varying teeth per inch, and whatever else you can find. Many of these, however, will be superfluous if you have a good power saw.

- Miter box – the steel kind, with a capacity for any angle, is best, but the wooden type is fine for 90° and 45° – the most common ones.

- Glue injector – actually a syringe made of metal or plastic which forces glue into difficult places. Useful for loose veneer and inseparable joints.

- Electric grinder – mainly for keeping tools sharp, an important requirement for furniture work.

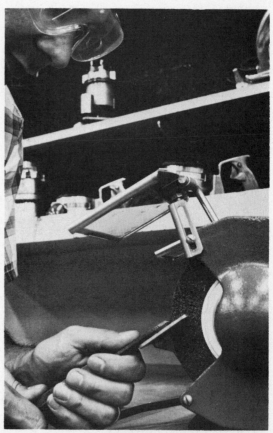

Fig. 3-13. It is important to keep chisels in good condition by sharpening them on an electric grinder.

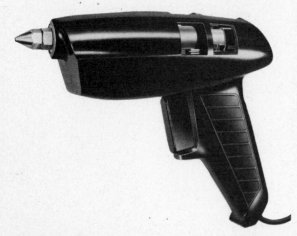

Fig. 3-12. A hot glue gun injects glue into difficult places.

Refinished sideboard.

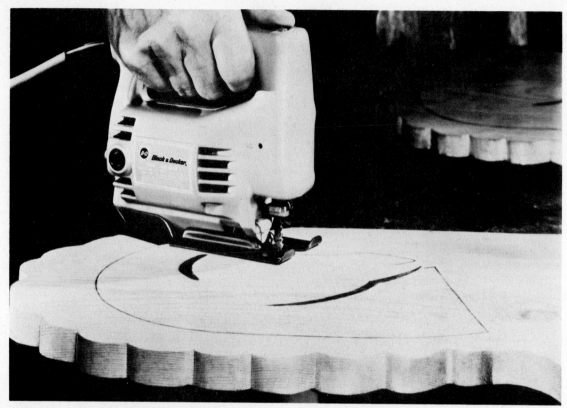

Fig. 3-14. A sabre saw is particularly good for cutting curves and cutouts.

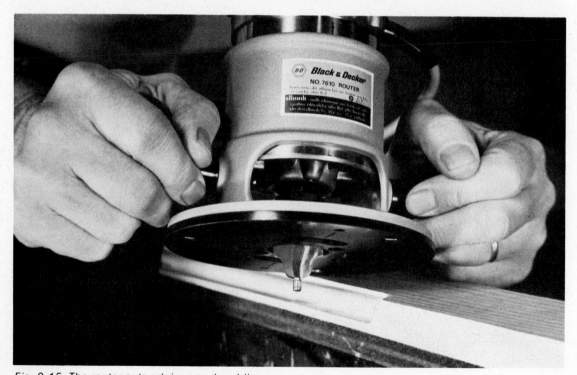

Fig. 3-15. The router cuts edgings and moldings.

- Spoke shave – a small plane with ears, which works by being drawn toward you. Indispensable for close work.

- Chisels – for wood, of course. Necessary items if you want to practise joinery.

- X-Acto knife – maybe it's made by other companies, buy they aren't too well known. If you're handy with a razor blade, you won't need these, but there are lots of uses for these different-shaped blades.

- Vise – woodworking or with woodworking jaws. Holds things steady when even a third hand couldn't.

- Sabre saw – if you have one of these and a 1/4-inch drill, you can throw the keyhole, compass and coping saws away. Will cut almost any line, but particularly good for curves and cutouts.

- Router – for edgings, moldings.

Finishing

- Tack rags – you can make your own, but it's easier to buy a few at the paint store or auto shop. Used for final wiping of a piece before varnishing to remove lint, dust and other foreign bodies.

- Swab sticks – sold in drug stores as ''Q-tips'' or other brands. Used to make ''pick sticks'', for removing small pieces of dirt and other offending specks from a newly varnished surface.

- Rubbing blocks – like a sanding block, only a little more flexible.

- Rubbing pads – hard felt about an inch thick, used for the final finish with abrasive powders.

- Spatula – for applying patching materials and stick shellac.

- Alcohol lamp – for heating spatula and putty knives without leaving soot on the blades.

- Varnishes, stains – same comments as under ''essential'' materials; just add to supply as you go along.

Fig. 3-16. Tack cloths are used for final wiping of a piece before varnishing.

3-4. Specialty Tools and Materials

Some of these may be essential for your use, some may not. If you do even minor upholstery jobs, for example, you'll need a tack hammer. On the other hand, if you stick purely to repair and refinishing of wood, you really don't need any of these. Tools listed for repair and refinishing that are also used for upholstery are not repeated here.

a. Upholstery

• Tack hammer — a must for an assortment of jobs.

• Staple gun — sometimes used instead of a tack hammer, but you'll find ample use for both. (Not an office-type stapler.)

• Shears — good quality, sturdy enough for cutting through heavy materials. It's not a bad idea to have another small pair for lighter material. (Left-handers should get a special left-handed pair.)

• Webbing stretcher — for pulling the webbing (and sometimes fabric) tight.

• Webbing — roll of burlap or plastic material used for seat and back reinforcement, holding springs and similar tasks.

• Assorted tacks and nails — all sizes of plain and fancy tacks, common nails and staples for tying cords and things to the wood.

• Manila or hemp string, tying twine — oddly enough, for tying strings.

• Heavy flax cord (1/8-inch diameter) — for fastening springs, webbing and other parts together. You may need some other specialized cords too, like mattress twine.

• Small metal straps — for fastening springs to wood.

• Padding — both foam and cotton, or any other kind you like.

• Muslin — for the underside of chairs and sofas.

• Upholstery needles — some standard sewing needles can be used, but large needles, straight and curved, are necessary to sew through heavy upholstery fabric.

• Fabric — this is expensive and is usually bought when needed. If you intend to upholster a great deal, you may want to have a few of your favorite cloths on hand, but ordinarily not.

b. Cane, Rush, Splint

These specialized techniques require no special tools except for pegs and clamp clothespins. You will, of course, need materials. All the following are available at chair-seating and specialty stores:

• Caning material — the best and only material for a long time was *rattan*, a palm stem from India, Ceylon, Malaysia and the People's Republic of China. The best cane comes in long, select lengths up to 20 feet. Sugar or bamboo cane, although suitable for some jobs, is not strong enough for chair-seating. Plastic cane is also acceptable if not as authentic-looking.

• Rush — can be bought at specialty supply houses, but you can also get your own by raiding the nearest swamp during August or the few weeks on either side of that month. Find some cattails with long narrow leaves (about seven feet long) and cut the stalks just above the ground or water. Pull off the leaves carefully, air for two to three weeks in a dry, dark, breezy room and they're ready for use.

• Fiber rush — this is the same as the rush described above except that it is made from a very tough grade of paper into rush-like form. It comes in varying widths and colors.

• Splint — long, very thin strips of native ash and hickory or tropical palm trees. The tropical palm strips are cut from the same tree as *rattan*. Here, the center or core material is split into strips and called "reed". Both are used similarly, except that reed is a little easier to bend, and true splint makes a better-looking seat.

• Macramé cord — this can be almost anything that will tie: polished cotton, sisal rope, India twine, Hong Kong grass.

c. Painted and Decorative Finishes

As used here, this type of finish is a highly specialized, difficult art which takes more natural talent and a keener eye than the finishes described elsewhere. Some of the effects are stunningly effective, however. The

Finished chair.

basic materials are listed here, with some of the techniques summarized in Chapter 4 of Volume 16. Those seriously interested in this type of art should procure a copy of *The Art of the Painted Finish for Furniture and Decoration* by Isabel O'Neil.

- Japan colors — available at some art-supply stores, but often difficult to find. If not available locally, write T.J. Ronan, 749 East 135th St., Bronx, New York, 10451. Basic colors are:

  Liberty red medium
  Signcraft red
  Chrome yellow light
  Green medium (Coach Paint)
  Green light (Coach Paint)
  Raw umber
  Burnt umber
  Raw sienna
  Burnt sienna
  French yellow ochre
  Lampblack

- White poster paint — mixed with the japan colors to provide lighter shades.

- Solvent and diluents — some will be the same as those recommended under "refinishing", but you should also add "flatting" or soybean oil, japan dryer and liquid detergent Triton X100.

- Brushes — most will be the same as those used for refinishing, except that you'll need more and better artist brushes. Number 3 and 6 long-haired point sable are the basic decorating brushes.

- Palette knife — used for blending colors.

- Many other ingredients are used to achieve the many decorative effects possible for painted furniture. Lacquers, casein paste, ox gall, kaolin powder, India ink, aniline powders, and other obscure materials will be needed as the art progresses. (See Chapter 4, Volume 16.) If you get involved in specialties like mosaic tile, you'll need special tile nippers.

One of the subdivisions of decorative furniture arts is gilding, which employs pure gold leaf. At one time the most popular and attractive of the techniques, this art is threatened by the rise in the price of gold.

3-5. The Importance of Adhesives

There is no factor more important in the repair process than the proper selection and correct application of adhesives. As you progress in furniture repair, you will find that certain adhesives are more to your liking than others. No matter how beautiful your repair job is, that finely finished coffee table isn't worth much if it collapses under the weight of a glass.

Due to the proliferation of trade and brand names for the various glue products, selection of the proper glue is often difficult. Consequently, a knowledge of the generic types is usually helpful.

In general, there are two types of glue: those formulated from materials of natural origin and synthetic-resin glues. The latter

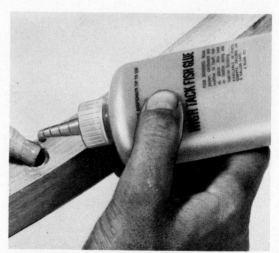

Fig. 3-17. Proper selection and application of glues is essential.

have been developed over the past four decades by the chemical industry. Ordinarily, furniture does not require a waterproof glue, although it is helpful if the glue is water-resistant, as many are. If the furniture is to be used outside, then the glue must be waterproof.

3-6. Effect of Product Construction

The choice of glue depends first of all on the conditions under which the glued product will be used. These are generally either normally dry for interior use or damp or wet with direct exposure to the weather for exterior use.

Wood shrinks and swells with changes in its moisture content — an appreciable amount across the grain, but generally only an extremely small amount along the grain. These dimensional changes across the grain are almost twice as large for flat-grain stock as for vertical-grain stock. Consequently, the stresses on the glue joint between two flat-grain pieces of lumber glued together with the grain at right angles (cross-laminated) will be very large with appreciable changes in moisture content. The stresses are cut almost in half if the pieces are vertical-grain; and if the grain in the two pieces is parallel (laminated construction), the stresses are generally insignificant in comparison to cross-laminated construction.

If the layers of wood are thin (veneers), such as in plywood, the stresses exerted are greatly reduced, and glue bonds can be made that will perform satisfactorily even under severe moisture changes. As an example of the effect of veneer thickness, a flush door having 1/8″ oak face veneers is more apt to develop glue failure between faces and crossbands than one having 1/24″ faces of oak, because the magnitude of the stresses on the joints will be greatly reduced when the thinner veneer is used.

It is very important, therefore, to design a joint so that the stresses will be held to a minimum under changing environmental conditions. If this is not possible, a glue that suffers the least damage under continued or repeated stress must be selected.

3-7. Wood Species

There is a wide variation both in density and shrinkage characteristics between the different species of wood. A combination of high density and high shrinkage results in the greatest stresses on the glue joints. Conversely, a low-density species having small shrinkage develops low stresses on the joints.

A criterion for a good glue joint in which side grain is bonded to side grain is that it should be as strong as the wood (fail in the wood when the joint is tested). A weaker glue bond that would suffice for a weak- or low-density species might not do for a higher density species. For example, a glue that performs well on a medium-density softwood might not be adequate for a high-density hardwood.

3-8. Surface Protection or Finish

Deterioration or weakening of glue bonds may be caused by a variety of factors. Exposure to moisture, heat, and shrinking and swelling stresses are all known to cause degradation of certain types of glues. A good finish (having high moisture-excluding effect) can significantly retard moisture changes in the wood, reducing shrinking and swelling stresses. At the same time, it provides appreciable protection for the glue bonds. The ability of good finishes to reduce the rate of moisture changes of glued wood products is often overlooked as a means of prolonging the useful life of glue joints. In selecting the proper glue, the type and durability of the finish is an important consideration.

The restored brass hardware on this writing desk gives it added elegance.

Fig. 3-18. White liquid glue is practical and versatile for furniture repair.

3-9. Characteristics of Glue

The temperature at which glue sets (room temperature, or lower or higher than room temperature) is an important factor in proper selection of glues. Pot use (usable life after mixing), storage life, ease of spreading, and ease of equipment cleanup are other factors that must be considered. The time between spreading and pressing and the length of time the joint must be under pressure are other factors that generally play an important role in the selection of a glue.

3-10. How Important Is Cost?

Since prices of glue are continually rising, it is impractical to list exact figures. Cost increases, however, from the relatively inexpensive soybean and vegetable glues to the animal, casein and synthetic-resin glues, and finally to the straight resorcinol-resin glues, which are the most expensive. Cost must be considered, however, in terms of actual cost per pound of mixed glue, and of the amount of glue spread required; that is, the cost to spread a certain joint area. Waste due to short pot life and costs of the equipment needed must also be weighed in comparing glue costs.

But the most important consideration in the selection of a glue is this: *will it give satisfactory performance for the intended use*? Considering the time spent on this type of project, the cost factor of even the most expensive glue is negligible.

3-11. Glues of Natural Origin

The glues formulated from materials of natural origin include animal, vegetable, casein, soybean and blood glues.

Animal glues, also called hide glues or hot glues, are probably the oldest known type of wood glue. They are made from the hides, bones, sinews and fleshings of cattle. Most animal glues come in a dry form and are prepared for use first by soaking in water, and then melting; they are applied while hot. Liquid animal glues, ready to use at room temperature, are also available (see below).

Animal glues come in different grades. The higher grades are preferred for joint work, while the lower grades are suitable for veneering. Hot animal glues develop strength first by cooling and jelling and later drying. They are preferred for hand spreading on irregularly shaped joints and for assembly work. The chief disadvantages of these glues are their low moisture resistance, the importance of temperature control in their use, and their relatively high cost.

Vegetable (starch) glues are usually made from cassava starch. They are sold in powder form and may be mixed cold with water and alkali, although heat is commonly applied in their preparation. These glues are relatively cheap, and remain in good working condition for many days. The normal vegetable glues prepared from powder are extremely viscous and it is not practical to spread them by hand. Special liquid glues, although easier to spread, are more expensive and are somewhat unpredictable.

Vegetable glues set relatively slowly, mainly by loss of water to the wood. In the past, vegetable glues were widely used, particularly for veneering, because the time between spreading and pressing could be varied without affecting the quality of the joint. The use of vegetable glues is limited today because they lack moisture resistance, like the animal glues, and because they cause staining in thin veneer. These glues have not been used extensively for joint work.

Casein glues are made from casein curd (protein) precipitated from milk either by natural souring or by the addition of acids or enzymes. Lime and other chemical ingredients are added to the casein to prepare the glue for use. Formulas are available for compounding your own glue from raw casein, but it is generally more convenient to use the prepared glues supplied in powder form, which require only the addition of water before use. The prepared glues are available in small retail packages. The many casein glues available include glues with long pot life but relatively low moisture resistance, and glues with good moisture resistance but definitely limited pot life.

Casein glues have sufficient strength for either veneer or joint work, although with high density wood species, the glue bonds are not as strong as the wood. They are used cold (although they may be hot pressed), and when properly mixed can be spread with a brush. The moisture-resistant casein glues are intermediate in moisture resistance, superior to vegetable and animal glues, but poorer than most synthetic-resin glues. The disadvantages of casein glues are their tendency to stain veneers, the relatively short working life of some types, and the dulling effect of the gluelines on tools. Each of these limitations may be minimized separately by special formulations, but generally at the sacrifice of some property.

Soybean (vegetable protein) glues, which are similar in general composition and characteristics to casein glue, are formulated from dried protein of soybeans. They are cheaper and generally produce lower-strength joints than casein glues and are therefore mainly used for veneering primarily of the softwood species. Soybean glues are not normally suitable for hand work or small shop operations. Their moisture resistance is generally somewhat lower than that of casein glues.

Liquid glues originally were made from heads, skins, bones, and swimming bladders of fish, but most recently they have also been prepared from animal-glue bases by special treatments. These liquid glues tend to vary considerably in quality from sample to sample, but the better types produce joints comparable to those of hot animal glues. Liquid glues are more expensive than other nonresin glues and are primarily used in small-scale operations, such as assembly or hobby work.

3-12. Synthetic Resin Glues

Synthetic resin, or simply resin, glues of various types have been introduced as woodworking glues since the early 1930's, but the greatest progress in their development began during World War II and is still increasing. These resin glues are products of the chemical industry and originate from raw materials that are derived from coal, air, petroleum, natural gas and water.

All resin glues described here, except the conventional polyvinyl-resin emulsion glues, are thermosetting types. They undergo irreversible chemical curing reactions to produce insoluble, infusible glue films in the joint. The polyvinyl-resin emulsion glues are thermoplastic; that is, they do not undergo any chemical curing during the gluing process but remain in a reversible state and soften on subsequent heating.

Some resin glues are sold in a single package ready to use or as a powder to be mixed only with water. Many others, however, must be prepared for use by mixing resin, catalyst, fillers, extenders, and water or other solvent at the time of use. In any case, the manufacturer's instructions should be followed closely.

Plastic (urea) resin glues are available in powder and liquid forms to be used with or without added catalysts, fillers and extenders. These glues are formulated for curing at room temperature (usually considered as about 70°F.) or at hot-press temperatures of 240° to 260° F. (not for the do-it-yourselfer). The gluelines are colorless to light tan and have only a moderate dulling effect on tools.

Urea resin glues have high water and moisture resistance at normal room temperatures, but are sensitive to elevated temperatures and degrade more rapidly as the temperature increases, particularly with high humidity. These glues are not for exterior use. Resistance to high temperatures and exterior conditions can be somewhat improved, however, by modification with special fortifiers. When properly formulated, the unmodified urea resin glues give high initial strength and are suitable for both veneering and joint work. They are generally not recommended where poorly fitted joints and thick gluelines are involved.

Resorcinol and phenol-resorcinol resin glues are dark reddish in color and are generally supplied as liquids to which a liquid or powdered curing agent is added before use. These glues have much the same performance characteristics, including high durability, as resin glues. They have the added advantage of curing sufficiently for many applications at low room temperatures. They are, however, among the more expensive of the current woodworking glues.

Recent formulations of phenol-resorcinol resin glues are much lower in price than straight resorcinol resin glues and appear to retain most of the desirable characteristics of the resorcinol resins. They are formulated for different rates of setting, the faster ones for use in cool weather and the slower setting for use in hot weather. Intermediate setting types are also available. They are all used for laminating or assembly of articles where a high degree of durability to exterior and other severe service is required. Their relatively high cost prevents their use as a veneering glue except for special applications. Several brands of resorcinol-resin glue are available for small-scale shop work and are of particular interest to the amateur boat builder.

Polyvinyl resin emulsion glues (the familiar "white glues") are available in a ready-to-use liquid form that sets at room temperature to a colorless glueline. Unlike the other resin glues described, these glues do not cure by a chemical reaction, but set by losing water to the wood. They remain somewhat elastic and thermoplastic after setting, which makes their use in highly stressed joints inadvisable. The polyvinyl resin emulsion glues are useful, however, for certain types of assembly joints where their greater elasticity is an advantage over the conventional rigid woodworking glues. Within recent years special vinyl copolymers have been introduced. These have some thermosetting properties and greater durability than conventional polyvinyl resin emulsions.

Aliphatic resin glues are cream-colored liquids that harden to a tone similar to that of animal glues. They are high-tack types that set very quickly. Since they do not "creep" under pressure, they can be used on load-bearing joints. (Some resin glues can be used on such joints only if the joint itself actually carries the load.) Aliphatics can also be used to fill gaps in poorly fitted joints, since they do not crystallize or powder out. Aliphatics can be applied and will set at temperatures as low as 50 degrees. Aliphatic resins are water-resistant, but not waterproof.

Epoxy resin glues set by chemical action

Fig. 3-19. Epoxy glue is extremely strong: equal parts of resin and hardener are mixed to activate its adhesive properties.

and, since there is no problem of trapped solvent, can be used to join nonporous materials. Originally developed for bonding materials other than wood, they have been found useful in woodworking. Because they do not shrink appreciably on curing, they can be used in thick gluelines. These qualities make them useful for projects which utilize different materials, such as wood and metal or glass.

Epoxies are among the strongest wood glues available, but they are in the higher price range. They come in two-part formulation and must be mixed before use. At normal room temperatures, the mixture has a working life of about two hours. Total setting time is about 18 hours, but this can be accelerated by the application of moderate heat, such as from a lamp.

All the glues described here are available under various brand names; your supplier should have at least one of each type. Whichever you use, there is one final point that must be stressed: *Read the manufacturer's directions, and follow them to the letter.* Even the strongest glue won't affix a postage stamp if it is not used in the way it was intended to be.

3-13. The Place where You Work

It is important in furniture work to have a warm, dust-free place to work. Glue, in particular, needs warm conditions; varying temperatures and moisture conditions will affect your wood adversely. Many varnishes, shellacs and other materials won't perform except within a certain thermometer range. A heated basement is ideal for a workshop; a heated garage is acceptable too.

3-14. Workbench

A big, old-fashioned workbench is not only a great place for working on chairs upside down, but also a convenient place to store tools. Perforated hardboard in back of the bench is useful for storing hammers and saws; and a few shelves will hold the finishing materials. A 2″ × 4″ strip at the back of the bench will keep things from falling off the back; you can drill holes in it to hold such tools as bits, brushes and screwdrivers.

3-15. Work Platform

A work platform is helpful because it raises the piece you're working on to a manageable height, and it provides a level area (if you build it right) for checking the evenness of chair legs, for example. By covering with a rug, you protect your work from being scratched or dented.

To make a work platform, first construct a frame about four by three feet square and about two feet high. Make sure it's level. It's a good idea to place the back next to a wall so that you can have something to push things against when you need pressure, such as when installing homemade wedges.

Fig. 3-20. Platforms are easy to make and handy for sanding.

Cover the 2″ × 4″ frame with a sheet of 3/4″ plywood or boards if you prefer. Cover the plywood with a piece of carpeting tacked around and under the outside of the frame.

The platform is a convenient place for stripping and refinishing, too. Cover the rug with newspapers when using messy materials like paint remover.

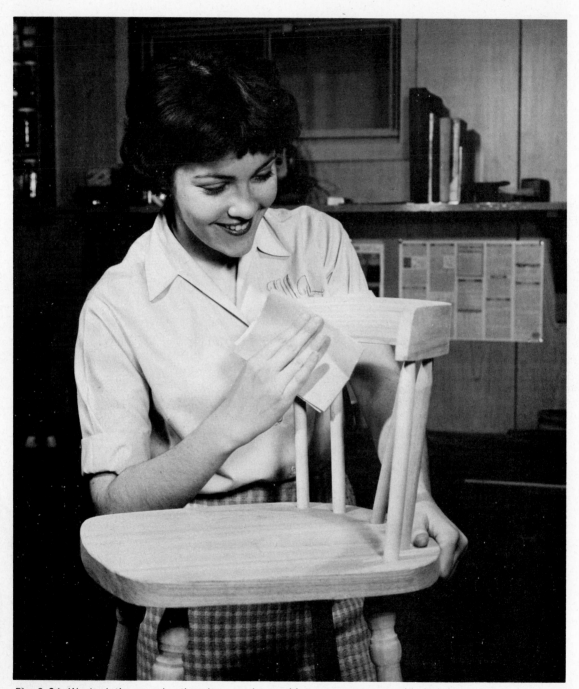

Fig. 3-21. Work platforms raise the piece you're working on to a manageable height.

Furniture Styles and Their History

It isn't necessary to know that a certain piece of furniture is an early Chippendale or late — or even that it's Chippendale. A chair can give just as much pleasure whether or not you know it's a ''Cornucopia-back Hitchcock''.

But as you get into furniture, you naturally develop a curiosity and interest in the types and styles of furniture, and in how and when they were constructed. Knowledge increases and sharpens our enjoyment of things, and it is in the interest of pursuance of pure knowledge that this chapter is written.

It would be a serious mistake to assume that such knowledge is necessary to produce a good-looking repair and refinishing job (although it's helpful if you're interested in ''restoring'' a piece in the strict sense of that word — making it look like it was in the beginning). You can take any old piece and make something nice out of it without having the foggiest notion of furniture style. So, if you're bored with styles and designs and want to get to the meat of the work, skip to the next chapter. That concerns furniture construction, which is something you must know.

4-1. The Fickleness of Style

Another word for style is ''fashion'', and if you know anything at all about fashion, you know that it changes from year to year. Furniture styles are like clothes fashions, too, except that the cycles of change are a lot more durable. As we write, the current fashion is ''eclectic'', which means that anything goes — as long as you like it. Theoretically, you can mix anything with anything: an Early American chair next to an ornate sofa, or a Spanish table with modern chairs. Bad as it sounds, it works out, apparently, in practice.

But eclecticism is new, and was preceded by a Spanish or Mediterranean craze, which in turn was preceded by both modern and colonial preferences. Yet, while all these fads were going on, furniture manufacturers were making other styles as well, which goes to show that not everyone follows the mob. You can't afford to with furniture. It's something you expect to have for a long time, through numerous fads.

4-2. The Older Styles

In the last few centuries, reigning monarchs have dictated furniture styles. The *Georgian* style is named after the early English King Georges, and the various *Louis* styles after the French monarchs. In the earliest known days, however, furniture was designed by

Fig. 4-1. The current fashion is "eclectic"; the roughness of a Castilian table is combined here with elegant, upholstered chairs.

craftsmen strictly for its utilitarian value, with a little style thrown in if possible (particularly in early Egypt).

It wasn't until the Middle Ages that a conscious attempt was made to create stylized furniture. From the twelfth to the sixteenth centuries there was only one style, and it was called by the general term *Gothic*. Religion was the dominant theme in men's lives and the furniture style was decidedly ecclesiastical. What was in the church was also in the home. After all, most of it was made in the monasteries. Greatly influenced by current architecture, Gothic furniture was ornate, massive and much the same throughout the western world.

Most furniture of the period was made of oak and was characterized by deep moldings and pointed arches. Wrought iron locks, hinges and straps abounded. The universal furniture piece, dictated by the exigencies of the nomadic times, was the coffer, an all-

Fig. 4-2. From the twelfth to the sixteenth centuries there was only one style of furniture, the Gothic, which was ornate and massive.

purpose chest used for sleeping, seating, dining and storing valuables. There were also throne-like chairs, trestle tables, joint stools and benches, but the few remaining other pieces — hutches, sideboards and cupboards — were simply variations of the coffer.

Toward the end of this period, however, the Renaissance was coming into full bloom. Having begun in Italy, it had spread to France and Spain. The glories of the ancient cultures of Greece and Rome were admired and imitated. During this remarkable period a humanistic philosophy evolved generally that recognized men as individuals. Although there was no revival of classical furniture as such, the Renaissance spirit demanded that

furniture designers model their works after what was best for man. New ideas of harmony and beauty required things that were compatible with Renaissance man, furniture that was more elegant and graceful.

As the Renaissance spread to Holland, Germany and then England, an improved economic climate meant that the new middle class had money to spend on furniture and other amenities of life. In at least its rudimentary form, every type of furniture imaginable was created in this era (1500-1700).

Although there were individual nuances to the various Renaissance pieces, the styles were basically similar, with some differences based on the country of origin.

4-3. Late Renaissance Elaborations

As the Renaissance drew to a close around the end of the eighteenth century, there were several styles that evolved as elaborations of the basic style. On the Continent, the most cherished deviations were the bold, forceful baroque and the more delicate, graceful rococo.

4-4. Traditional and Provincial

"Traditional" generally means those styles that were favored by the monarchs — hence, society — of their period. "Provincial" refers to the type of furniture that evolved from the provinces. In some cases, these were crude imitations of the traditional; in others, they were less elaborate and more classically simple. These are named after the country of origin. "Contemporary" furniture is somewhat of a misnomer, since it means the furniture that is being built today (or in recent years) regardless of what the style is. In other words, the starkly modern acrylic table and the heavy oak chair can both be classed as contemporary if they are manufactured in the present period. "Period", incidentally, is another confusing word ordinarily synonymous with "style".

For our purposes, these somewhat arbitrary classifications will be played down, and the emphasis placed on the various styles from both country of origin and chronology — more or less ("more or less" because many of the styles overlapped). Virtually all furniture you see today, old or new, dates from one or more of the late and post-Renaissance styles outlined below.

4-5. Early English

There has always been a distinctly British style of furniture. This was particularly true during the seventeenth to nineteenth centuries, when furniture makers from England gave us a multitude of pleasant styles.

The early English styles date back to the late Renaissance and the reigns of the famous royal families:

Jacobean (1603-1649) — also known as "Stuart", covering the reigns of James I and Charles I. It is masculine, massive and bold. Wood is extensively carved and primarily of oak. Square and rectangular lines are dominant. Decoration is very ornate.

Commonwealth (1649-1660) — also known as "Puritan", which describes it better than "Commonwealth". The style was a violent reaction against the "corrupt" Jacobean. Straight and severe lines dominate, with little or no carving or other decoration. Square shapes predominate, with high, straight backs and low seats. Stout underbracing (very practical) and somber-hued upholstery was the order of the day.

Carolean (1660-1688) — also known as "late Jacobean" or "Restoration". Restoration comedies were very popular in this period, and the risqué sophisticated style of this type of drama is analogous to the furniture. It was a return to early Jacobean influence and, coincidentally, the monarchs bore the same names as before — James II and Charles II. Features were elaborate: deep carvings, spiral turnings or twirls on legs or strechers, with molded panelling. Oak is still predominant, with some walnut. Cane seats were common, and rich tapestries were used for upholstery.

William and Mary (1689-1702) — Mary Stuart's husband, William, was a Dutchman who, upon acceding to the throne of England, brought to that island the craftsmen and styles of the Continent. The graceful and subtly styled furniture combined straight and curved lines in a harmonious manner that was as well suited for a home as it was for the king's castle. Walnut began to take over from oak as the most popular wood and upholstery was much more extensively used than before. Decorations featured the "inverted cup" at the tops of legs, with flowers, cupids and wreaths as carvings. Much of this was gilded, painted and lacquered.

Fig. 4-3. Identify the style of this desk and chair by consulting Figure 4-11.

4-6. Traditional English

The term "traditional" English furniture is usually applied to those styles developed during the great upsurge of the art of furniture-making in Great Britain during the eighteenth century. Many of our most popular styles date from this time.

Queen Anne (1702-1714) – this period is often said to have produced the first "modern furniture". The "cabriole" leg, curved and ending in a foot, was an ever-present feature, as were undulating lines and a trend away from elaborate ornamentation. (Scallop shells were a favorite theme.) Comfort is beginning to be a factor, with the "overstuffed" chair coming into its own. Brocades and embossed leather are the favorite materials. Walnut is the chief wood, with some oak, ash, pine and mahogany.

Georgian (1714-1820) – this period was marked by the reigns of the first three King Georges, famous in American history as well as English. English furniture-making evolved to such a high degree during this time that for the first time several of the craftsmen have their names attached to certain styles. The period is also known as the "Age of Mahogany", since new tariff laws allowed heavy imports of this reddish tropical wood, and furniture manufacturers used all they could get. Other general features are the predominance of curves over straight lines and the influence of French and Oriental styles. Rich upholstery and gilding are common. The masters of the period were:

- Thomas Chippendale (1718-1779) – heavily dependent on carved decoration, delicate and intricate or bold and lavish, depending on the piece. Familiar motifs are shells, lions' paws, the leaf-like acanthus, acorns, roses, scrolls and dolphins. Chippendale wrote the first *Directory* of furniture-making, which is still consulted today.

- Robert Adam (1728-1792) and James Adam (1730-1794) – primarily architects, these brothers designed furniture for the houses they built. Heavily influenced by the Greeks and Romans, their style was classically simple, restrained and delicate. Straight, slender lines with flat surfaces are common, with sparse, low-relief ornamentation. Dainty, carved moldings and urns are most common features.

- George Hepplewhite (d. 1786) – built things on a smaller scale than the others, with graceful, refined and slender lines. Distinguished by serpentine fronts and concave, cut-in corners. Graceful curves are combined with sturdy construction. Restrained use of dainty carvings, with wheat ears, urns, rosettes, ferns and other classical motifs.

- Thomas Sheraton (1751-1806) – really a designer, writer, teacher, bookseller and sometime fanatic more than a craftsman. He would create a piece and turn it over to others to produce. His designs were delicate and refined, and much sturdier than they appeared. His pieces are well-proportioned, with straight lines dominant. Inlays are used more than decoration. Carvings utilized urns, ferns, ovals and floral swags. Sheraton was fond of mechanical devices such as trick springs and secret locks.

4-7. Later English

No master craftsman has approached the fame and beauty of design since the four masters of the eighteenth century. There have been several styles in vogue in England, however, since that time. These are generally referred to as:

English Regency (1811-1830) – not to be confused with the French Régence period discussed below. This marked a return by the British to simplification and functionalism with a great deal of foreign influence. The French *Directoire* and *Empire* styles (see below) were much admired and copied. The Orient, particularly China, was extensively studied, with most of the pieces now being covered with lacquer (a Chinese trademark). Black was the favorite color, with white and ivory as occasional alternates. Gilding was very common. Furniture was scaled down to small, intimate sizes. Curves were simple, bold and combined with straight lines. Chinese motifs were the favorite, carved and in relief.

Victorian (1830-1890) — the long reign of Queen Victoria is well known for solemnity, primness and sentimentality. Furniture was no exception. Designs were heavy, substantial, often clumsy. Both upholstery and wood were dark and usually dreary. "Stuffiness" is a word commonly applied to the era and its furniture, yet some of the pieces have a quaint charm, and the best examples are very good indeed. Black walnut and rosewood became more popular than mahogany.

4-8. Early French

The French have always had a flair for design and decoration that sets their work apart from that of the rest of Europe. French furniture is characterized by a delicate sense of balance, attention to fine details, skill in carving, inlay and painting techniques.

Louis XIII (1610-1643) — marked mostly by straight lines, squares and symmetrical designs. Prominent decorations are twisted columns, broken pediments, inlays, elaborate carvings, spiral legs and turned balusters. Ebony, walnut and oak are the principal woods.

Louis XIV (1643-1715) — the lavish court life of the period is reflected in the heavy, massive, baroque furniture encouraged by this luxury-loving and long-reigning king. Dominated by straight lines, chairs are high-backed, carved and upholstered. Under-structures are elaborately carved and heavy on all pieces. Walnut, oak and ebony are favorite woods.

French Régence (1715-1723) — the massive forms of the previous era were supple-mented by rococo ornamentation, which was lighter and more airy. Fantastic curves and elaborate — sometimes eccentric — designs were the rule.

Louis XV (1723-1774) — the ornate and luxurious rococo style came into full flower during the half-century rule of Louis Quinze. At the same time, however, Louis XV furniture is smaller and more delicate in scale than that of earlier styles. The women closest to the king, Mesdames de Pompadour and Du Barry, led the trend to more comfortable, intimate and feminine styling. Small desks, chaise longues, and occasional tables came into being during this time. The extremely fancy designs of this period included a multitude of curves, cabriole legs, carved knees and scroll feet. Louis' personal *Bureau du Roi* (king's desk) is reputed to be the most elaborate piece of furniture ever built. Its decoration included carvings, metal inlays, ormolu (gold-like) mounts, painted panels, gilt and lacquer. Favorite woods of the day were mahogany, oak, walnut, chestnut and ebony.

Louis XVI (1774-1793) — in spite of the fact that this was the last reign of the aristocracy before the French Revolution of 1789, furniture saw a gradual withdrawal from the florid style of the previous Louis. The discoveries at Pompeii and Herculaneum of classical ruins prompted a revival of chaste, unadorned simplicity. The furniture of the period toned down the flair that characterized the prior decades, just enough to bring out the best of the style. Refinement and elegance were the bywords, with curves giving way to more straight lines and classical motifs emphasizing the authority and beauty of line. Mahogany was the pre-eminent wood, with some rosewood, ebony and tulipwood.

Directoire (1795-1804) — The Revolution changed both life and furniture styles radically. Under the rule of the five directors (*directoires*) following the Revolution, the Jury of Arts and Manufacturers ruled public tastes in furniture, among other matters. The trappings of royalty and aristocracy were eliminated and replaced by classic and military ornaments. Furniture is straight-lined,

Fig. 4-4. (A) A delicate antique French Provincial love seat is one of the principal attractions of this room;

(B) French Provincial furniture mingles perfectly with the contemporary background of shag carpeting.

graceful, elegant and pure.

French Empire (1804-1815) — during this period, which saw the rise and fall of Napoleon I, furniture again became ponderous and ostentatious, but the period was dignified by classic restraint and simplicity. Furniture finish began to receive new importance, with sheen and high polish replacing some of the more gaudy forms of decoration. Roman eagles, torches, lions and wreaths were the dominant symbols, surpassed in their stateliness only by the more obvious "N" enclosed in a victor's wreath. Rosewood and ebony were used in addition to the still popular mahogany.

4-9. French Provincial

The evolving French Provincial style covered a period of approximately two and a half centuries from 1650 to 1900. This style began as a practical and functional art, with the pieces designed simply to meet the needs of the French farmer. During the latter part of the period, however, the peasant styling drew its inspiration more and more from the salons of Paris. The result is that pieces from the diverse areas of Normandy, Provence, Burgundy and elsewhere began to take on a certain similarity to the traditional styles. These designs were far less heavily ornamented than the Louis designs they copied, and used local, more readily available woods like oak, walnut, ash, poplar and fruitwood. Later, well-established French Provincial styles are often preferred by experts over the court styles. They are simpler, more comfortable and less pretentious. The designs and ornamentations varied from province to province, with the common feature being more streamlined versions of the gaudier Parisian creations. Some of the common characteristics were panelling and carving, which replaced the inlay of Paris traditional, large locks, oversized hinges and other metal decorations.

4-10. American Colonial

The more popular lay term for furniture of this period is Early American, but as far as the experts are concerned the correct name for the style of furniture made in pre-Revolutionary days is "American Colonial".

Early Colonial (1620-1700) — a hybrid style transported to this country by the early settlers from their homelands. The first New Englanders were Puritans and their furniture was plain and utilitarian, a sturdy, simplified and more severe version of the Jacobean styles back home. All of the early colonial pieces were crude but efficient, and constructed out of whatever wood happened to be around. Pine, birch, maple and walnut were the most common.

Late Colonial (1700-1790) — another name for the period is "American Provincial". As the period began, the emerging American colonists were rejecting the designs of local cabinetmakers and importing furniture from England. American craftsmen in the cities began to reproduce Queen Anne, Chippendale and Sheraton pieces for the well-to-do, and very fine designs developed as the craft progressed. This type of furniture is formal and sophisticated and is really more traditional and provincial. The great cabinetmaker of the day was Duncan Phyfe (1768-1854). Phyfe's shop in New York City became famous for lyre-back chairs, pedestal tables and curved-base sofas with flared legs and lion's paw feet. Phyfe drew his inspiration from the works of Sheraton, the Adam brothers and Hepplewhite and later from the works of the American Empire or Federal style (see below). Phyfe used mahogany almost exclusively. His designs are finely proportioned as well as structurally sound. Prominent motifs, in addition to the ubiquitous lyre, were acanthus, cornucopia, lion's heads, medallions, wheat and leaves of palm, oak and laurel.

American Empire (1795-1830) — also known as "Federal". Duncan Phyfe was also dominant here, but there were other themes that this style drew on, mostly French Empire.

Fig. 4-5. This elegant bedroom furniture is in the Early American style.

Fig. 4-6. The drop-leaf table was popular in Early American furniture.

Fig. 4-7. The massiveness of this credenza and chair would seem to indicate it is a copy of the older styles.

The American versions of their European counterparts were heavier and sturdier. Motifs are similar to the late Colonial except that patriotic motifs such as eagles became more and more popular.

Pennsylvania Dutch (1680-1850) – this popular American style spans two centuries and is traced to the German immigrants (incorrectly called "Dutch" as a perversion of *Deutsch*) of eastern Pennsylvania, New Jersey and southern New York. These were solid Germanic pieces, simple and plain. Decoration was primarily in the form of colorful painted motifs similar to the "hex" signs so popular today. Woods were locally available varieties such as maple, walnut, pine and fruitwood.

Shaker (1776-1850) – the Shakers are a Quaker off-shoot, and share the Quakers' rigorous convictions. Thus, Shaker furniture is severely functional, handmade and totally lacking in decoration. Paint or stain was occasionally allowed, but usually a light coat of varnish was the only "decoration". By the same token, the Shaker devotion to hand work produced excellent craftsmanship, appealing symmetry and line. They used native pine mainly with some maple and other hardwoods.

4-11. Italian Provincial

Italian Provincial styles lasted from about 1700 to 1850. Like French Provincial, the style originated diversely in scattered rural areas and then began to copy some of the better features of traditional design. Italian Provincial owes more to the early baroque style than some others. Local craftsmen kept the large, bulky scale, while eliminating the lavish decoration. The lines of this style are predominately rectangular with straight, taped, square legs and unornamented, sparse curves. Main forms of decoration are paint, enamel, moldings and brass hardware.

Walnut, mahogany and fruitwood are the popular woods.

4-12. Biedermeier

Germany has certainly not been the cradle of furniture design that other European countries have, but there was a brief burst of activity in Germany during the early half of the nineteenth century. The stolid German middle-class was rejecting the baroque and rococo styles that emanated from the rest of the continent. Local designers began producing their own versions of French Empire and Directoire furniture, but severely simplified and stripped down. The name "Biedermeier" was humorously attached to the style after a fictional German character named "Papa Biedermeier", supposedly the typical bourgeois German. These pieces are quite varied, again because of various places of origin, but common features are functional design, plainness, sparseness of ornamentation with reliance on native fruits, flowers and painted details. Woods are birch, maple, ash, fruitwood and mahogany.

4-13. Other Styles

There are, of course, many other furniture styles. Those interested should read some of the many fine books on the subject. Mediterranean, for example, recently enjoyed a huge burst of popularity. This rather vigorous, masculine style is a throwback to the Moorish domination of the region, of which there are few remaining authentic artifacts outside museums. The more modern styles (usually of pecan) are not usually the subject for refinishing, because they aren't old enough. The same holds true for many different modern and contemporary styles. Not only are they too new, but some are made of plastic and other materials that are not really "refinishable".

Fig. 4-8. Much contemporary furniture does not use wood as its primary material.

Fig. 4-9. This lounge chair is in the contemporary Danish style.

Fig. 4-10. In the future, furniture as we know it may disappear entirely, as in this space-age boy's bedroom.

4-14. How to Recognize Styles

The descriptions and drawings in the previous sections will help you pick out certain styles, but overlapping of styles and periods is bound to cause confusion. The best way to recognize many types of furniture is by the chair and leg shapes. The accompanying chart is a guide to some of the more readily identifiable styles. Do not assume, however, that a certain piece is ''genuine'' because it has the proper characteristics. The best styles have been — and will continue to be — frequently copied.

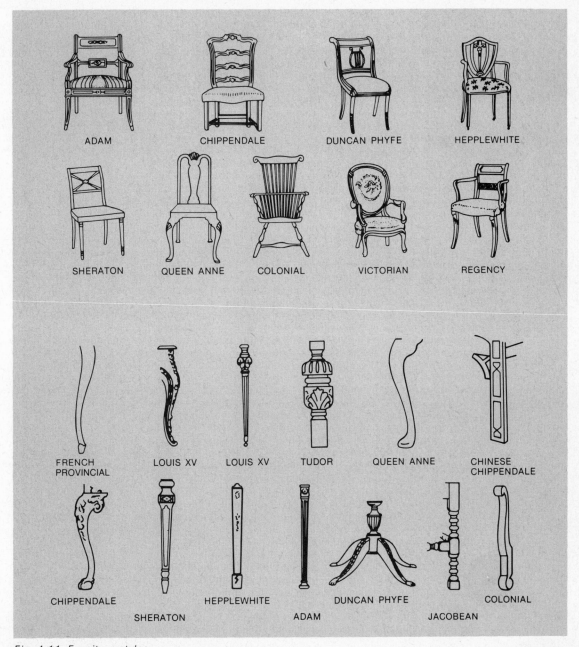

Fig. 4-11. Furniture styles.

Rudiments of Construction and Structural Repair

If a piece of furniture is in very bad repair, you have several choices. You can throw it away, give it to a pro to fix, convert it to something else, or take it apart and fix it. It's an individual choice, and it depends on how valuable the piece may be and how energetic you are.

There's not much anyone can say about the first two choices. You either do or you don't. There's a lot someone could say about the third choice, such as how to convert an old round table to a cocktail table, but this is also a very individual thing and depends on the particular piece in question. We can, however – and will – say a bit about choice four.

Perhaps the first question is whether the piece has to be taken apart. Generally, the answer is yes, assuming it is in bad repair. Something that needs just a new finish or has a loose rung can be fixed without going to extremes. A chair or table in poor shape, however, is almost impossible to fix without taking it apart and seeing how it was put together.

5-1. Basic Construction

Fortunately for all of us, furniture-making is a simple, if demanding, art. There is something clean and simple about wood, though. Turn a table over and a quick examination will tell you how to take the top and legs apart. There's nothing mysterious about it. The top is attached to a frame and so are the legs. Find the screws and glue blocks and remove them.

5-2. Joinery

The key to effective furniture repair is an understanding of the art of joinery. Being able to take down and repair the joints of furniture is what separates the men from the boys. Before you can do that, however, you should know how the joints are put together.

There is an infinite variety of joints used in furniture building and cabinet making. All have the same purpose – to make a joint as strong as possible, able to withstand the stresses and strains of normal usage, while remaining as unobtrusive as possible for esthetic reasons. (It goes without saying that all joints are held together with glue.)

Plain-edge or butt joints are the simplest of all joints and also the least satisfactory for most purposes. Nails or screws must invariably be used to insure holding. These joints are rarely used in furniture construction and, when they are, the edges must be carefully checked for square before the pieces are fitted together. It is essential here that all mating surfaces be perfectly joined.

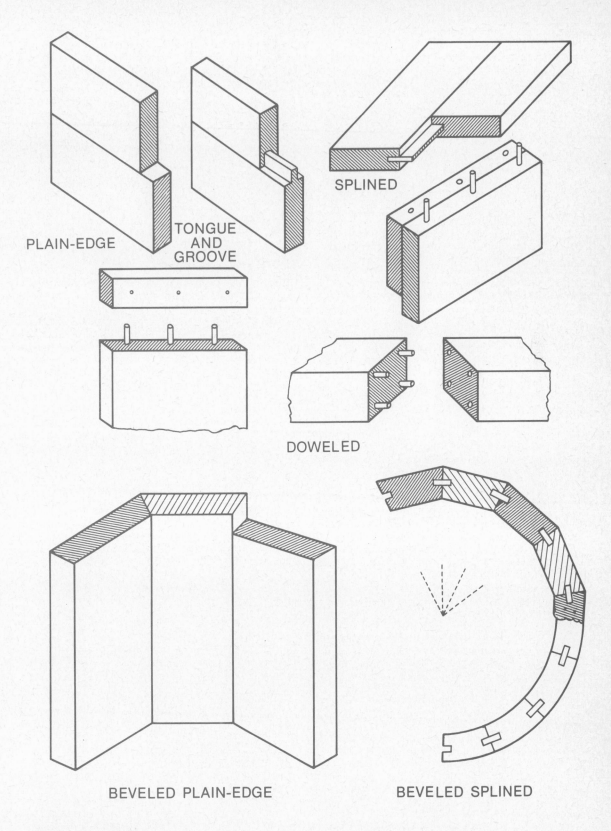

PLAIN-EDGE

TONGUE
AND
GROOVE

SPLINED

DOWELED

BEVELED PLAIN-EDGE

BEVELED SPLINED

Fig. 5-1. Wood joints.

Halved or lap joints of various types are commonly used in such areas as shelves, cabinets and chair stretchers. They are easily made by first laying one piece of wood on top of the other and accurately marking the width of each cut. A try square is then used to square these lines across both work edges, and to square the shoulder lines of both the face and the edge of the workpieces. A marking gauge is ordinarily used to indicate the depth of cut.

With the workpieces secured in a vise, a backsaw is used to cut to the required depth. If wood notches more than one inch in width must be cut, it is advisable to make several cuts to maintain the accuracy of the depth. A chisel is then used to remove the waste down to the proper depth. The cuts can then be filed to a uniform depth for a perfect fit.

Rabbeted joints are formed by cutting recesses (or rabbets) on the edges of the workpieces so that they may be fitted into each other. They are used in cabinetry, table tops, and other constructions that utilize long joints. The rabbets are cut by marking a squared line across the face of the work and down the edges, corresponding to the thickness of the joining piece. Depth lines are marked on the edges, and the scrap material is then cut out.

Dado joints consist of a groove cut into a board into which another board is fitted. There are several variations, the most common of which is the housed dado. In this joint, the entire end of the piece to be fastened fits into the groove of the main piece. The piece to be fastened is set on the other piece and the width of the cut is marked and squared. The depth of cut is then marked and the cut made with a backsaw. Scrap is removed with a sharp chisel.

Other types of dado joints are the stopped

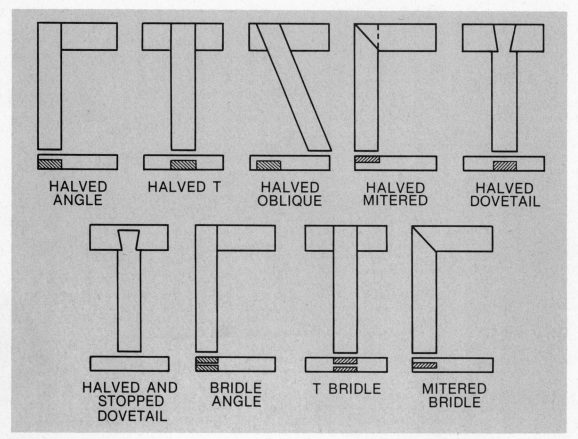

HALVED ANGLE

HALVED T

HALVED OBLIQUE

HALVED MITERED

HALVED DOVETAIL

HALVED AND STOPPED DOVETAIL

BRIDLE ANGLE

T BRIDLE

MITERED BRIDLE

Fig. 5-2. Wood joints.

dado, in which the groove does not extend the full width of the board, the dovetailed dado, and the dado-and-rabbet.

Mortise and tenon joints are favorites with skilled cabinetmakers. They are strong and dependable, but must be fitted accurately. They are widely used in the construction of desks, tables, chairs and cabinets of fine quality.

Again, as can be seen from the drawings, there are several variations of this joint, but all are laid out and fitted in the same general way. The tenon, or male, end is made first. Both workpieces are then cut and squared to the desired dimensions and both faces of each piece are marked for easy identification. The length of the tenon is measured on the appropriate piece, then a square is used to mark this shoulder line around the piece. A rule of thumb is that the tenon should be a quarter to half as thick as the entire piece.

The exact center of one edge of the piece is measured and, using this center point, the outline of the tenon is scribed on this edge. The lines across the end of the piece and down the other edge are carefully scribed. The tenon's width is marked in the same way.

The piece is placed in the vise and a backsaw and chisel are used to cut the tenon. The position of the piece is changed around so that all cuts will be made square. The shoulder cuts are made last.

The length of the mortise must equal the width of the tenon. If you are making such a joint yourself, locate the exact center of the piece and, working from there, lay out the mortise. Carefully check the dimensions against those of the tenon.

When you are satisfied that your layout marks are correct, fix the piece in the vise. Select a drill or auger bit 1/16″ smaller than the width of the mortise, and adjust the bit

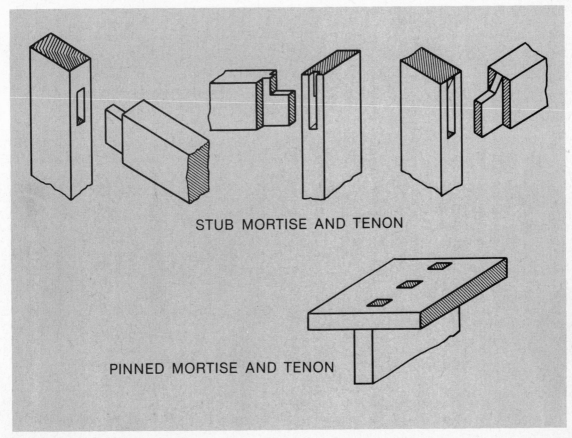

STUB MORTISE AND TENON

PINNED MORTISE AND TENON

Fig. 5-3. Mortise and tenon joints.

gauge to bore 1/8″ deeper than the length of the tenon. Place the spur of the bit on the center line and bore a series of overlapping holes with the two end holes touching the end lines of the mortise. Make sure the bit is kept perpendicular to the face of the workpiece. Use a sharp chisel to clean out the scrap in the mortise and to trim the sides and corners, keeping the walls of the mortise perpendicular to the face of the workpiece.

Dovetail joints are also favorites of skilled woodworkers, especially in such applications as drawers, and in furniture projects where strength and good appearance are important. The flare of the projections (called pins) fitting into matching dovetail must not be too acute,

as this would defeat the purpose — an acute angle would be weakened by the short grain at the corners of the angle.

Making dovetail joints requires a certain skill and it is suggested that the amateur woodworker practice on scrap wood before tackling an actual project. (You can also buy a jig for your power saw.) A template of cardboard or thin wood is used to lay out the dovetails after the proper angle has been decided. Cuts are made with a backsaw and sharp chisel. The common-lapped dovetail, through dovetail, and lapped dovetail are the most commonly used. Actually, dovetails are nothing more than sophisticated mortise-and-tenon joints.

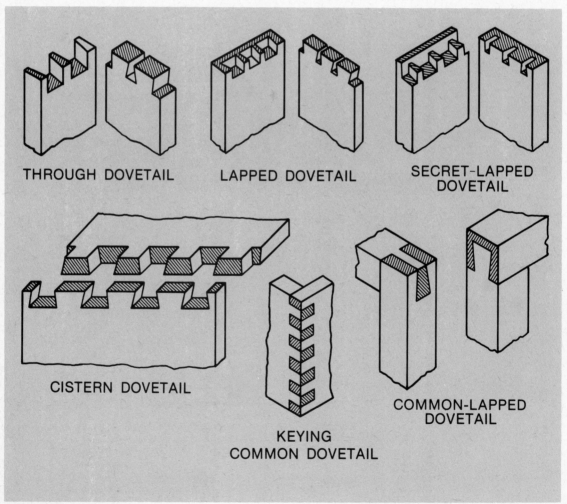

THROUGH DOVETAIL   LAPPED DOVETAIL   SECRET-LAPPED DOVETAIL

CISTERN DOVETAIL

KEYING
COMMON DOVETAIL

COMMON-LAPPED
DOVETAIL

Fig. 5-4. Dovetail joints.

Fig. 5-5. Making a dovetail joint with router and template.

Miter joints are used primarily for making frames and screens. They are usually cut at an angle of 45°. While it is a simple matter to mark an angle of 45°, it is usually more satisfactory and safer to use a miter box to cut the workpieces accurately — or else cut the boards on a table saw or radial saw with the gauges properly set for the angle.

Since the miter joint is simply a butt joint cut at an angle, dowels, tongues, or braces are often used to strengthen it. To make a tongued miter joint, grooves are cut in each of the pieces and a wooden tongue is glued into the groove. In addition to strengthening the joint, this also helps to prevent warping.

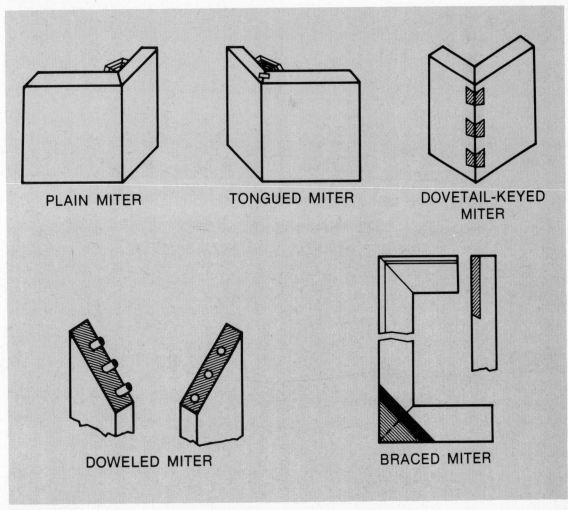

Fig. 5-6. Miter joints.

5-3. Doing It Yourself

Making complex mortise and tenon and dovetail joints is fun once you get the hang of it, but it is not an easy art to learn. Patience is required, particularly if the parts are hand-made. Power equipment and the appropriate jigs will help, if you have them. Many of these cuts can be made with a circular saw, jointer, drill press or router. If you buy these tools, the manufacturer's instruction booklet will usually show you how to make the joints. If you no longer have the book, Rockwell has an excellent series on how to use these various power tools. *Getting the Most Out of Your Circular Saw and Jointer* has a very good chapter on how to make wood joints. Consult your Rockwell dealer or write the company at:

Rockwell Manufacturing Co.
Power Tool Division
550 North Lexington Ave.
Pittsburgh, Pa. 15208

On the other hand, there is no real need to know how to make all these joints yourself. You should know enough about them to be able to take them apart and put them back together again. You should know how to reglue and strengthen them if necessary. Once in a while, you may have to fabricate a new piece and connect it to an old one. If the joint is a complex one, you can always take it to a cabinetmaker and let him do it, saving your energy for other chores. You're going to need it.

Actually, most joints that will need repairing are simpler ones where an arm goes into a back, or a rung into a leg. The dovetail and other difficult joints rarely fall apart precisely because they are built to last.

5-4. Before You Start

It's tempting to pick up that wooden mallet and give everything a whack to see what's going to fall apart, but don't do it — not yet. Before you take things apart, take a good look at the piece and see what you're going to have to do.

A thorough inspection is the best way to plan your work. Here are some of the things to look for:

- Unless the thing looks almost perfect, it's a good idea to make notes as you proceed. Many of those who do a lot of repair work have a platform which serves several purposes (see Section 3-15). One of them is to provide a stable, level surface to see whether the legs are even. It is also a good place to rock the frame and locate any loose joints. Look for any missing parts and, while you're at it, search all surfaces for holes, cracks, gouges or dents. The veneer should be inspected for blisters, cracks and loose edges. Note any warped boards.

- Open drawers, doors and other moving parts. See if slides must be fixed, hardware replaced, joints repaired or hinges fixed.

- Look at the piece overall with a jaundiced eye. See if any of the parts detract from the overall good looks and consider removing them. Would it look better cut down? Many older chests have high legs which might look better a few inches lower. Might some parts look better painted than varnished? Ask yourself similar questions. Try to imagine what it is going to look like when it's finished, and make any changes first. There's nothing more frustrating than working on a part for hours and then deciding to get rid of it.

5-5. Taking Things Apart

Now comes the fun. Working from your check list, knock apart all loose joints, remove parts to be discarded or replaced, take off all hardware except hinges (and if they're shot, take them off, too). Put the hardware in a safe place. Use a wooden mallet for pounding or wrap some rags around a claw hammer.

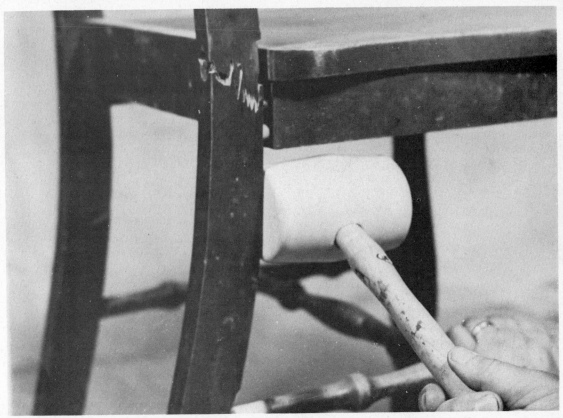

Fig. 5-7. Before knocking apart the piece, study it to determine exactly what you must do.

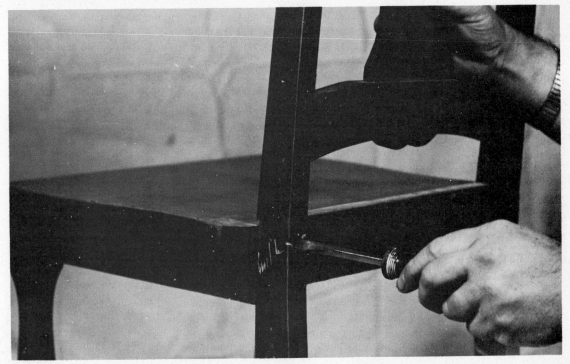

Fig. 5-8. A joint may be held together by hidden screws.

You may find, however, that the old joint won't come loose with normal hammer blows. If so, don't hit harder without looking more closely. The joint may be held together with hidden screws or nails in addition to the glue, or it may be one of those old-fashioned joints where a piece of dry wood was fitted with a small knob on the end, then inserted into a piece of green wood, which then dried and shrank. This made a fine, tight joint at the time, but over the years it tends to loosen.

For the chair with the hidden hardware, look for buttons or round plugs which may be hiding the screw head. Remove the button or plug as carefully as you can to get at the screw. As far as the old knob joint is concerned, you really shouldn't remove it all, because you'll have to force it and the knob won't fit right afterward. The best way to fix this is by forcing glue into the loose joint with an oil can, squeeze bottle or ordinary toothpick. You can also use a "glue injector", a tool available at specialty shops, and force the glue into the joint through a 1/16″ hole drilled in an inconspicuous place.

5-6. The Right Glue

Chapter 3 describes the types of glues available, and when each of them is best for certain jobs. What, however, is the best all-round furniture glue? Talk to a dozen cabinet-makers and you'll get at least a half-dozen different answers. Some will use nothing but hot hide glue, others think Elmer's is just great. Casein is popular with many others. Others will tell you it depends on the job.

Following is a chart meant as a *rough* guide only. For specific jobs, consult the sections on glue beginning with Section 3-9.

- All-purpose indoor glue – hide glue. A bit old-fashioned, hide glue takes a little longer to set than other glues, but when clamped and dried properly, is unbeatable for general use.

- Light-strain areas – white glue like Elmer's (polyvinyl-resin emulsion). Easy and quick.

- Where high strength is needed but the joint is a little loose and needs filling – casein glue.

- Edge-to-edge gluing, other high-strain jobs with tight-fitting joints – plastic resins like Weldwood.

- Exterior usage – resorcinol.

- When all else fails – epoxy resins.

With a little persistence, you should be able to determine which glue is best for you (even second-best will usually do). But how to apply it? Whether you have to heat it or mix it depends on the glue, so consult the manufacturer's recommendations. But that's only half the answer. The other half lies in what you do before and after you apply the glue.

5-7. Preparation for Gluing

The best glue in the world won't work unless the surfaces are completely clean before application. This means that all old glue must be scraped or sanded clean before you put the pieces back together again. Your knife and electric sander will be useful here. Be careful, though, that in your eagerness to clean the piece you don't take off too much wood along with the glue, particularly if you use a power sander or a very sharp knife.

You should also be sure to work in a reasonably warm place. There is ordinarily no problem, but if your workshop is an unheated garage (and it shouldn't be), you'll be well advised to do your gluing in some warm corner of the house where this sort of work will be tolerated by others in the family – or save the job for summer. Most glues do badly in cold temperatures.

Before hammering legs with a mallet, be sure they are not attached with countersunk nails.

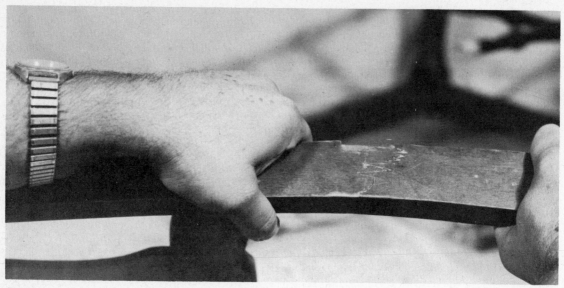

Fig. 5-9. It is important to apply the right pressure when gluing.

5-8. Pressure

In addition to having a clean surface, applying the right pressure is important when working with glue. The type of pressure depends on the job to be done. If you are gluing a chair leg into its socket, for example, or mending a broken one (a risky job at best), you should apply heavy weight downward on the chair seat.

5-9. Tourniquets

Applying downward pressure works well on seats and dresser tops which have a flat surface for stacking books on, but most repairs are more complex than that. Some sort of clamping is necessary for most repairs. That doesn't mean that you need a set of every clamp available. A piece of rope will prove to be one of the most valuable tools you'll have in your shop.

For all jobs involving side-to-side pressure, like the common rungs-and-legs repair, it is a simple matter of tying the rope loosely around the legs a couple of times, then inserting a stick between the strands. Twist the stick a couple of times until the rope is good and tight, then rest the end of the stick against one of the rungs or legs to keep it from flying back. Insert some rags or something where the ropes bite into the legs to prevent the rope from chewing up the surface. This type of clamp is known as a tourniquet.

5-10. Clamps

You will always find situations where one of the commercial clamps will be necessary. The more work you do, the more use you'll find for bar clamps, wood clamps and C-clamps. Pipe clamps are also handy for extra-long jobs. For them, you'll also need an assorted set of pipe lengths, threaded on one end to match the clamps. Clamps and pipe are available in either 1/2″ or 3/4″ sizes.

Wood Clamps

Use wood clamps to hold two small pieces

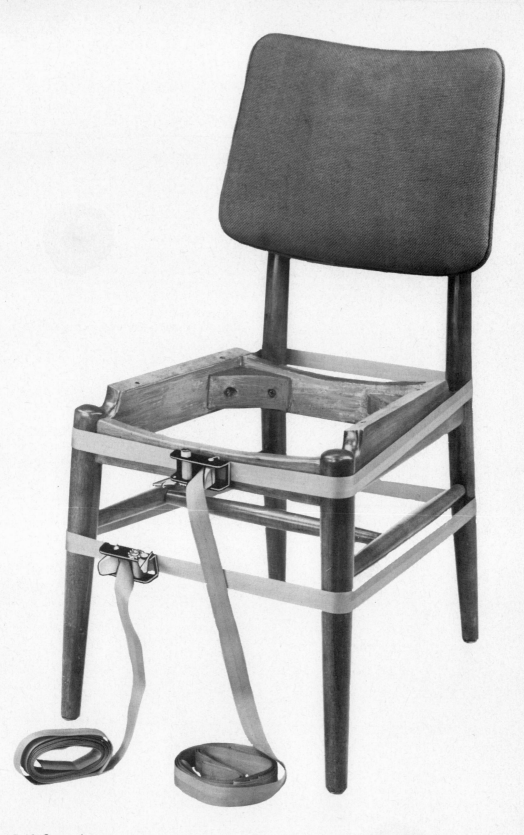

Fig. 5-10. Strap clamps.

Chair before being revived.

Fig. 5-11. Hand screws.

together, or to clamp one piece of wood to a larger piece where the distance is not great. Although these wood clamps come with jaw openings up to 15 inches, you'll probably use the smaller ones most often, substituting the bar or pipe clamps for longer stretches. The beginner is often puzzled by difficulty in opening and closing the hand screws. There is a quick and easy trick for moving the jaws to the proper width. Simply grip one handle in each hand and swing the clamp around until the jaw opens or closes to the desired distance.

To use the wood clamp, open to a width

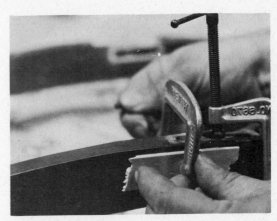

Fig. 5-12. C-clamps.

Fig. 5-13. Bar clamps.

slightly wider than the distance to be spanned, then tighten each screw until the wood grips evenly and firmly. Give the outer screw just a little more final twist for added tension. There is no need to use any padding between the wooden jaws if you don't apply excessive pressure.

C-Clamps

C-clamps are used mainly for small, spot jobs, such as gluing down a chip or repairing a broken chair rung. They come in many sizes, but the small ones are the most commonly used. These clamps have metal jaws and a thin piece of wood or other padding is necessary wherever the jaws bear against a finished surface.

Bar and Pipe Clamps

The serious repairman should have at least two bar clamps around. These come in very handy when spanning a fairly wide surface like the back of a dresser. The jaws are opened by sliding the movable section down the bar until it is just a little larger than the span to be bridged. The clamp is attached and the screw tightens the clamp until the proper pressure is applied. Pipe clamps are not self-contained, as the bar clamps are. When you buy pipe clamps, all you get is the ends. You have to buy the pipe to match, either from a hardware or plumbing-supply store. One end is threaded to hold the stationary clamp. The other section of the clamp is free to move up and down the pipe to span whatever width you need. The size of a pipe clamp, then, is infinitely variable and

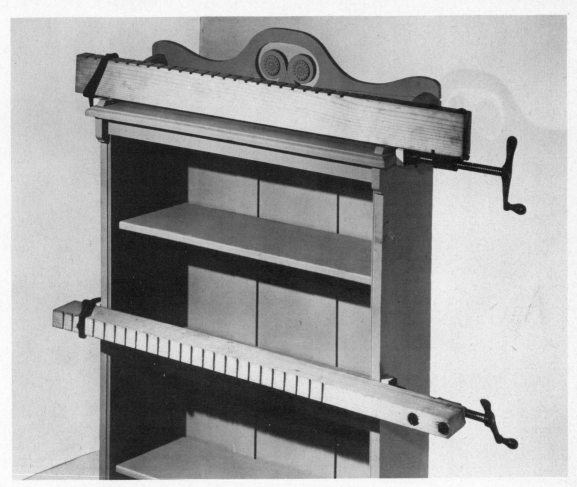

Fig. 5-14. Bar clamps.

limited only by the length of the pipe. If you think you have a job for a 100-foot clamp, you can manage it with a pipe clamp. Use wood blocks under both bar and pipe clamping to avoid damaging finished surfaces.

Other Clamps

There are such things as corner clamps, but usually you can improvise with one of the others. The only exception might be picture frames, where corner clamps made for this purpose are helpful in holding the edges firm until the glue dries.

You can also make your own wedge clamps, which are very useful for such jobs as binding boards together edge to edge.

Wedge clamps are made of a rectangular piece of fairly thick wood (3/4″ to 1″ is best), which is marked a half-inch from each edge and cut down the diagonal to form two almost triangular pieces. The pieces to be glued are laid on a wooden surface such as a subfloor or platform. The outside piece is braced against a wall or similar solid vertical surface. Put the two wedge pieces together as they were before cutting, then nail the outside one down, leaving the nail heads protruding slightly so you can pull them out later. Then force the remaining wedge between the other wedge and the work by tapping it with a hammer. If the wood to be glued is thin, weight it down to keep it from buckling under the pressure. Put wax paper under the glued area to prevent sticking.

Veneers and plant-ons.

Fig. 5-15. (A) Bar clamps holding moldings.

(B) corner clamps on picture frame.

(C) wedge clamps.

5-11. Specific Jobs

If you master the primary principles of furniture repair – surface preparation, proper gluing, clamping pressure – you should be able to repair almost any piece of furniture with a little ingenuity and luck. There are a few tricks, however, that go with every job. Here are some of them:

a. Loose Chairs (Lower Section)

Once the underpinnings of a chair start to go, everything seems to go with them.

The first thing to do is take apart all the parts that are loose. Then check to see if the parts will be tight when you glue them back together. The rung-to-leg joints will usually fit all right, but often the joint where the leg is fastened to the seat will have widened due to wobbling of the leg. No amount of glue is going to hold this unless the joint is tightened.

You may use wooden matches or toothpicks to fill the loose space.

Another way to expand a loose joint is by sawing a kerf down the middle of the leg top, filling with a hardwood spline just slightly larger than the kerf, and pounding it in until the spline pushes out the leg enough to fill.

If the thickness of the pieces to be joined

Fig. 5-16. a. Scraping old glue off chair rung.

Repairing scratch in dining table.

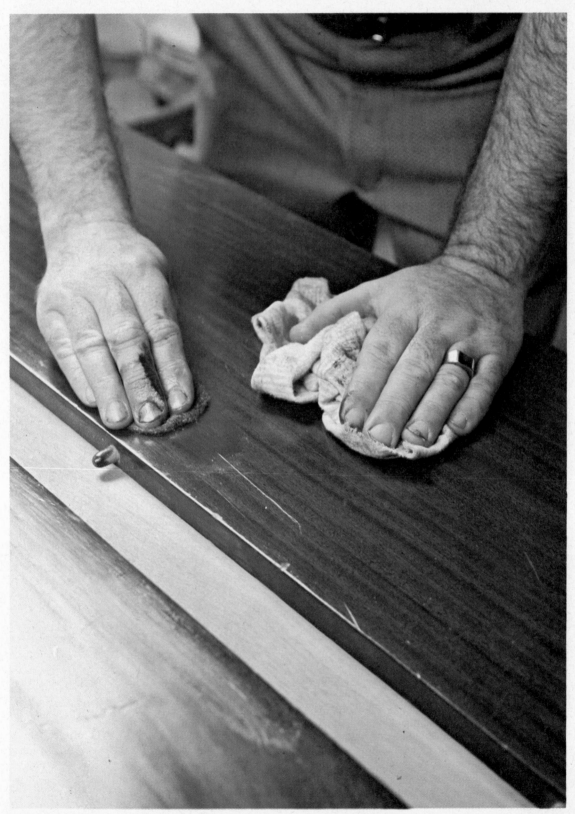

Repairing scratch with matching stain.

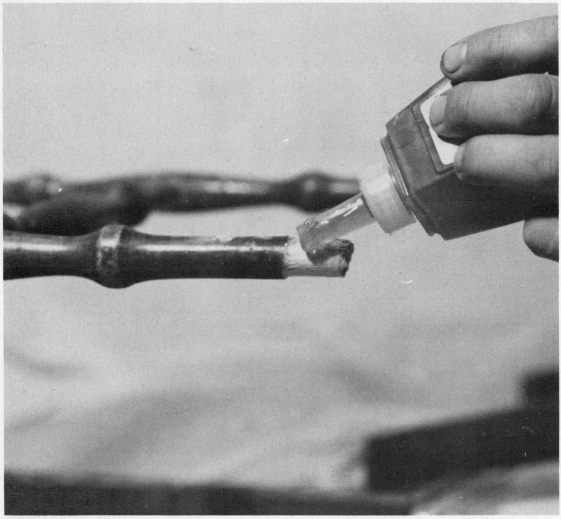

b. Applying glue to chair rung.

allows it, you can insert a dowel between the end of one piece and into the other. Drill the holes carefully with an electric hand drill or drill press and a bit of the same diameter as the dowel. Hold the wood very carefully to make sure that the holes are vertical. Grooved dowels offer the most glue surfaces and a tighter joint, but straight dowels are all right if used properly and roughened with a rasp.

Test the dowels to see if they fit tightly without binding. If the holes are misaligned, you're better off plugging up the old holes and drilling new ones. Once alignment is satisfactory, spread a generous amount of glue (casein is usually preferred here) and clamp the pieces together until dry.

Fancier chairs, such as dining chairs, will usually have stretchers forming a frame for the seat. This type of chair usually holds together better than the kitchen variety, but there are times when it too shows its age. In this situation, you'll probably have to remove and reglue corner blocks, and sometimes contend with screws holding the legs to the stretchers.

Dowels are often used, too, in this type of construction and are sometimes broken off. To remove old dowels, use an auger bit. New dowels are a must in this situation, as are new corner blocks where ruined. Otherwise, repair techniques are the same as for any other chair. If nothing else works, wood or metal braces may be added to produce the required strength.

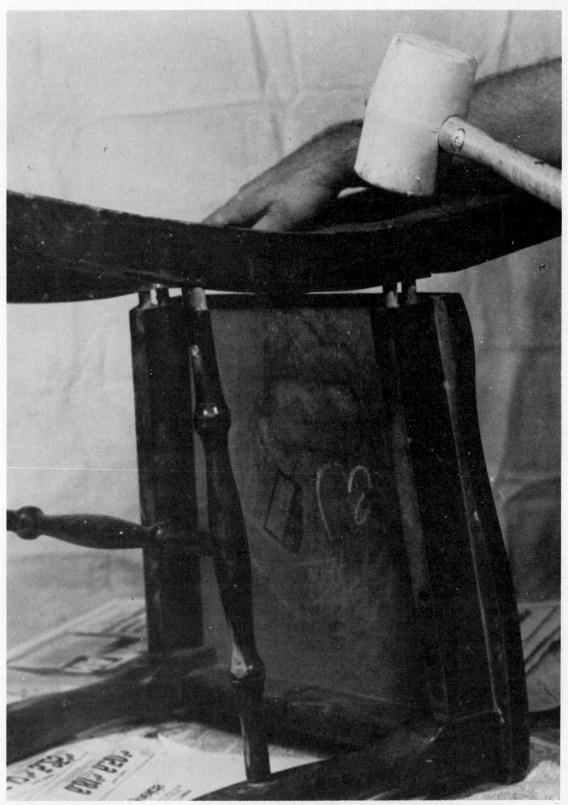

Fig. 5-17. *Beginning here and on pages 97, 99 and 100 are photographs showing the step-by-step repairing of a chair. Step 1.   Tapping dowels back in place with rubber mallet.*

Stripping old finish.

Step 2.   Applying cord for tourniquet.

b. Loose Chair Parts (Upper Section)

Wobbly arms are the main offender here, and their repair is a little tricky. Often, the arms are held in place with screws in addition to the glued joint. The biggest problem here is that the novice may not realize that the screws are present and he may wreck the joint by trying to pry it apart without removing the screws.

Screws holding chair arms are countersunk and often covered with wood buttons or wood plugs that have been cut off flush with the surface. The older and more skillfully finished the piece, the more these plugs blend in with the finish and are quite difficult to find. If the arm won't come out, however, with the usual whack or tug, don't ruin things by banging it around until it comes apart. You may find the entire chair in pieces.

When you run into this situation, you have to remove the button or plug and get at the screw. The button can be pried off with a knife or similar instrument and saved for replacing later. Removing the plug is a little tougher. Take your knife or a sharp awl and dig the plug out, which will ruin it, of course. You'll have to make a new one out of a dowel. Or simply fill up the resulting hole with colored wax or a shellac stick (see Sections 6-6 and 6-7).

After you expose the screwhead, the next step is to remove the screw. This may not be easy, but your chances are increased if you use a screwdriver which fits the slot perfectly. A good tool for removing stubborn screws is a screwdriver bit in your brace. You can bear down harder and apply more torque. Particularly stubborn screws will often loosen up if you jerk the bit quickly first left, then right.

Once the screw is out, the joint should respond quickly to a rap with your mallet. Clean and reglue as described above, filling the old screw hole with bits of scrap wood (or toothpicks and matches). You won't need clamps for this type of repair, since you will replace the screw, which does the same job.

Backrests of kitchen and Windsor-type chairs are often loosened in the same manner as rungs and legs. The same principles apply as working on the lower part of such chairs.

Here, though, the slats or spindles are usually installed with little if any glue, with the main outer rail taking the brunt of punishment. Devote your energies to strengthening the main members of the back and hope for the best with the spindles. Your toothpicks and matches should prove useful for chair backs as well as legs.

c. Broken Arms and Legs

Almost any broken piece can be put together again with proper gluing. The only exception might be chair rungs, where the biggest man on the block is sure to rest his foot and break the repaired joint. With a clean break, you don't have to worry about the old glue — but be sure the surfaces to be glued are clean and dry. Usually the break is partially longitudinal so that you have a fairly large surface to clamp together. C-clamps are the treatment of choice, one at each end of the break, with more in the center if there is space.

A broken part almost always loosens up the joints at either end of the part, so you may as well reglue these while you're at it. If you let the break go awhile, you may find that other parts have loosened as well. Tighten up everything at the same time, or your repair is doomed to failure. Don't forget to use thin wood blocks on either side of your clamp jaws. You'll also have to use either a bar clamp or a rope tourniquet to hold the loosened parts together while drying.

If the break is in the same place as an old one, be sure to clean off the old glue. Better yet, don't bother fixing it, since the second glue job will probably be weaker than the first. Chair rungs are easily fabricated from a similar wood dowel, but more complex parts will require a lathe or a cabinetmaker (preferably the latter) for replacement.

New parts are fitted the same way the old ones would be. You may have to shave the ends a little if they are too big or you may have to fill with scraps if the part is a little too small. Finish as any new part.

Chair legs often break right at the top where they join the seat. In most cases, the only

Step 3.   Tightened tourniquet applies pressure to the rungs.

realistic answer is a whole new leg, or a new piece scarfed into the old leg. In either case, you should probably go to a cabinetmaker— or, again, do it yourself with a lathe.

d. Missing Parts

When you find or buy an old piece of furniture, some of the parts may be missing. Simple

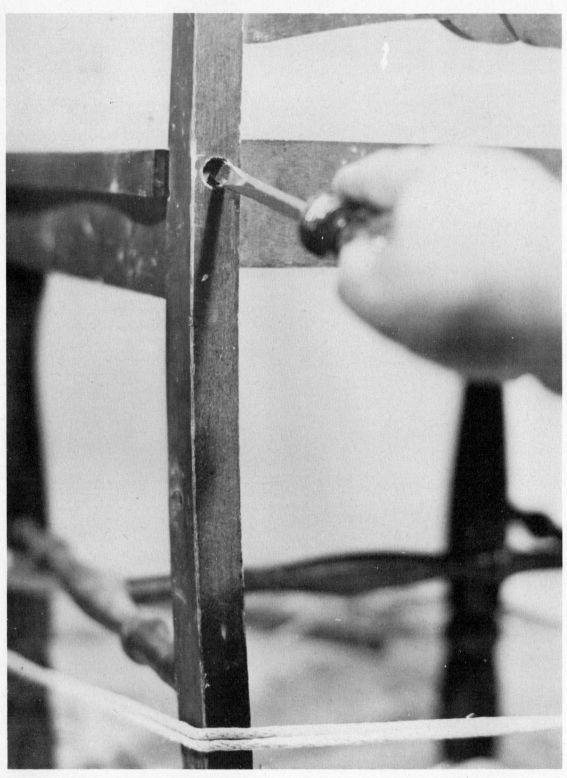

Step 4.   Tightening screws in chair back.

parts like rungs and other underpinnings you may construct yourself from wood of the same or a similar species (always use hardwood). There are several ways to approach decorative parts, which are another matter entirely.

● You can leave the part off. If it is not one of a pair, you may not notice that it's gone once you're through with the refinishing.

● You may be able to buy the same or a similar part in a secondhand shop, or find a matching part on another piece of furniture. Large cabinetmakers' shops may stock the part. The best source for those (and lots of other things) is Albert Constantine & Son, 2050 Eastchester Rd., Bronx, New York 10461. (Incidentally, you should

never throw away decorative parts that may be of some use later.)

● A drastic step, but one you may want to consider, is removing the matching part if it is the other half of a pair. On a high-back chair, for example, with a missing "rabbit ear" at the top of the back, it is possible to cut off the one on the other side. This may leave a somewhat bastard piece, but that is better than a lopsided one.

● The best way to provide a missing decoration if you can't find one is to have one made by an expert cabinetmaker. If you have the expertise, try tracing a pattern from the part you have, and cut another one out from a piece of similar hardwood.

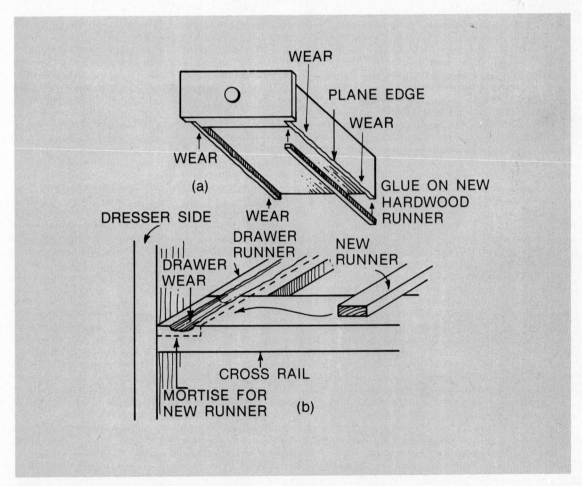

Fig. 5-18. Replacing runners on worn drawer.

You'll probably need some special wood-carving tools for this, and a lot of patience.

e. Sticky Drawers

Try to determine the cause before proceeding. Usually you'll find missing or broken drawer runners (bottom edges). You can replace these easily with a piece of scrap hardwood and some brads. Often, the cause is unevenness of the chest itself, which pinches the drawers and causes sticking. Check with a level and put something under the short legs. A little soap or paraffin on the runners may be enough to cure minor problems.

If the piece is old, you may find that the runners or guides (the boards which the runners ride on) are worn and uneven. Add thin strips of wood to worn runners. To fix worn drawer guides, rabbet out the old one until smooth, then shim up to their former height with rail strips. Easier methods are to install plastic bumpers or tape in the worn areas.

If the drawer itself is wobbly, check the joints. If they're dovetailed, gently tap the joint apart, being careful not to break any of the tenons. Remove old adhesive, reglue and clamp as described above. Here, corner clamps may be helpful to keep corners square. Other joints can be fixed in the same way, of course, but non-dovetailed joints will probably fall apart again under hard use. If possible, and the piece is otherwise valuable to you, replace the old joints with a dovetail.

f. Splits in Large Flat Parts

Usually caused by poor drying of the wood before assembly. Even a piece that has been around a good many years may crack and split if placed in a house with excessive humidity. Whether the problem is in a dresser top, bureau side, or table leaf, the solution is approximately the same.

Remove the part from its neighbors by unscrewing, removing glue blocks, or knocking apart. If a piece is only partially split, you

are better off cracking it all the way, odd though that may sound. A partial split is difficult to glue properly. If you complete the job that nature will probably finish anyway, you'll have some accessible surfaces to apply glue to. Properly glued and clamped, the split will be just as good as new — maybe better.

The thin panels found in the sides of chests or cupboard doors cannot be fixed in this way, but they are easily replaced by a piece of the same thickness. Note that these panels "float" in their slots and are not glued because they must have room to expand and contract with the moisture in the air. Still, they do occasionally split, particularly if the inside is not finished. To prevent such splits, give the inside a coat of linseed oil, sealer, varnish or shellac. This will help keep the moisture content the same on both sides.

Sometimes you can close up hairline cracks by removing the panel and soaking the inside with wet rags for a day or two, then nailing a thin strip of wood over the inside length of the split.

g. Warps

Warped boards are usually long ones like table tops, doors and similar large areas. The cause of warping is the same as that for splits and cracks — moisture. It is good to remember when doing your own refinishing that most warps could have been avoided by the simple expedient of applying a coat of some kind of sealer to the interior surface of the part. These finishing materials keep moisture out of the wood — at least, to roughly the same extent that the "finish" finish on the other side does. You should know that sealing the underside of a truly valuable antique may lessen its value. Antique experts like to be able to examine the bare wood.

In any case, it is the uneven moisture absorption that causes warping. The most effective cure is balancing the moisture by wetting the unfinished side and drying out the other at the same time, if possible. There are many ways to accomplish this: steaming the part or putting it over a radiator with wet rags on top are two of them. The best way seems to be laying the unfinished side on wet grass in the bright sun. Remember that the dry side is the one that curves in and should receive the damp treatment.

You must, of course, remove the top in the manner described under "Splits" above. If the warp is a "simple" one, in which the boards curve in the same general direction, use the grass method (or some other wetting gimmick). Sometimes the warp is more complex, however, with a "twist" longitudinally as well as a warp. If such is the case, put a big rock or other heavy weight over the part that is more out of shape than the others.

You should be able to see the effects of your labors in a few hours, or by the end of the day anyway. When the board is just about as straight as you can hope for, put it back where it came from as tightly as possible. Clamp any loose edges, as you would have for a table leaf, to a couple of straight dry boards to help keep it from warping back again. Some experts feel that it is acceptable to attach permanent cleats to the underside of table leaves that are prone to warp, while others feel that this destroys the value of the piece,

since cleats will be visible when the leaves are in place. Our preference is to try all else first, and use cleats only if the case is hopeless. Apply cleats, if you use them, immediately after taking the warp out of the board.

The wet method will work in most cases, but there are times when it doesn't. According to the experts, the warp in such cases is caused not by moisture absorption but by internal stresses in the wood, according to the way it was cut – radially or tangentially (see Chapter 2). With a power saw, cut a series of kerfs in the underside of the piece about three inches apart and to a depth of about 2/3 of the thickness of the board. Make wooden splines to fit the grooves, preferably in a slightly wedged shape. If the part is curved so that the kerfs are in the concave (edges curled upward) side, then tap the splines in slowly, forcing them into the glued grooves with a mallet. If the kerfs are on the convex (edges curled downward), cut the splines thinner and do not force them at all. Glue loosely and liberally into the saw kerfs. Clamp flat against some straight boards. Another, more effective way to cure warping is to cut the part into

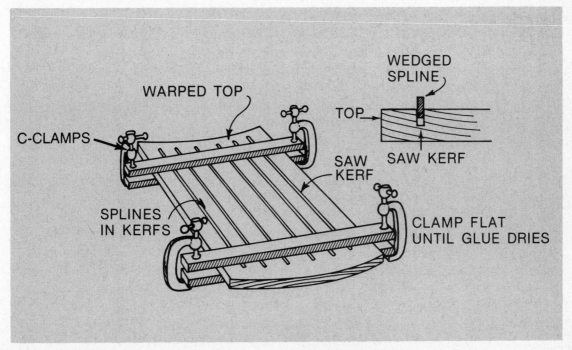

Fig. 5-19. Straightening warped top.

several small boards, and put them back together in an alternating pattern. This is delicate work, and usually ruins the looks of the top.

As soon as the cured part has dried out, screw or glue it immediately back where it came from. You may find, however, that during the wetting process, some boards have fallen apart. These will have to be glued back together by the method described under "Splits" above. This may be a good time to insert dowels in badly warped areas. Since there is a chance of drilling crookedly through the top, you shouldn't attempt it without a drill press or drill press attachment for a radial arm saw (see discussion of dowels below). Remember that minor warping is not always a bad thing. As a matter of fact, it is often prized in truly old antiques.

h. Loose Screws

Mainly a problem at hinges, where the weight of a door or leaf exerts constant pressure and sometimes pulls the screws out of their original tracks. In many cases, the screws point into table tops or the veneer, so that by using the time honored trick of replacing the loose screws with longer ones you run the risk of popping through the finished surfaces. Longer screws will work sometimes, but it is dangerous — you can't use them more than once. The use of larger screws is also limited by the diameter of the hinge holes. The best and easiest way to cure loose screws is to fill the screw hole with wood chips, splinters, toothpicks and glue. When the mix dries, the screw should go back in tightly again. When wood is too dry or splintery, or into endgrain, you may have to cross-bore from a relatively invisible spot and insert a dowel into the screw area. The dowel should be tight and well glued, and afford an excellent surface for the screw to bite into.

Alternate methods of tightening up screw holes are:

- filling hole with wood dough

- filling with epoxy putty

- filling with wood expander

All of these methods are acceptable. Which one you should use depends on the particular job at hand.

i. Working with Dowels

There are many cases where a joint, split or other defect can be strengthened by the use of dowels. Some of these have been indicated in the text, and other uses will come to you as you proceed. There are times when dowel work does not require a high degree of accuracy, as in many end-to-side joints. The beginner is urged to try his luck there, and not attempt using dowels to put together side-by-side boards in a table top as a first job.

When putting two boards together edge to edge, dowels are often of excellent value in adding strength and reducing warpage. To use dowels in this way, accuracy is vitally important. Any slight displacement of the dowel will result in unevenness which is difficult to correct.

Make sure to use grooved birch dowels for edge-to-edge work. You should also have a drill press — an electric drill at any rate — plus dowel pins and, unless you're experienced, a dowelling jig. The jig is set to certain dimensions and ensures that each dowel hole is straight and accurately bored.

After all the holes have been drilled in one side, insert dowel pins into each hole and very carefully line up the other side. Press the undrilled piece onto the pins and the point will indicate exactly where to drill into that side to ensure correct alignment. The holes on both sides should be countersunk to collect excess glue and provide greater strength. Use clamps, as always.

j. Patches

Chapter 6 covers patches of a cosmetic nature, like those used for veneers and to repair gouges and burns. Some experts can patch almost any part of a piece of furniture and make it look good. They can cut a part of

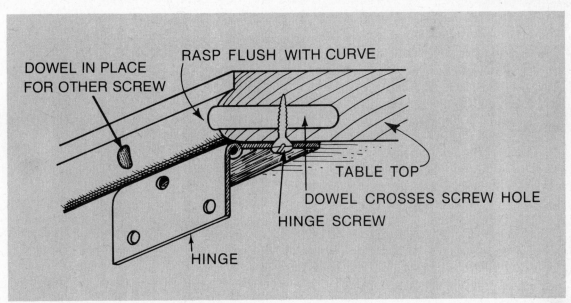

Fig. 5-20. Using dowels to fix loose hinge on table.

a chair leg, bureau top or desk surface, fit it, plane it, sand it, stain it and make it look like new. There may come a time when you can try this, too, but there are many easier things to learn first. If a structural part needs patching, our advice is to take it to a cabinetmaker — or don't bother with it. There are two exceptions to this:

1. *Mortise and tenon joints* — can be damaged due to hard wear. Since the tenon is invisible, you can usually do a decent job of patching. First, cut off the broken tenon, and make a second mortise where the old tenon was; be sure to match the mortise on the other side. Then make a new double tenon to bridge the gap and fit into the two mortises. You don't necessarily have to cut a blind tenon, even if the other one is. It's easier to cut all the way up to the top of the new tenon if you find the blind mortise too difficult. Fill the joint with plenty of glue (casein or hide) no matter how you cut it. If the joint is subjected to severe stresses, it may be wise to add small dowels across the sides into each end of the double tenon.

2. *Butterfly Patches on the Undersides of Chairs* — will often be the only cure for such things as split seats. First, cut the patches in the shape of a butterfly; then lay them over the underside of the two pieces in the positions they will occupy when put together. Trace the outline of the patch on the seat bottom and chisel out. Place the pieces together, glue all around and insert the butterflies. Clamp the patches down and clamp the pieces against each other.

6

Cosmetic Repairs— Restoring and Reviving

This chapter is concerned with the *appearance* of a piece of furniture — how to improve its looks, rather than its structure. It is assumed that the piece either has had its major structural alterations already or never needed any. It just looks bad. The veneer is broken or unsightly; there are gouges or bruises; or maybe it's just dirty.

Many beginning restorers assume that they'll have to strip the old finish off a piece of furniture to make the wood look decent. That is not necessarily so. Very often, years of neglect and abuse have simply built up a solid layer of dirt and grime. Before you commit yourself to the time-consuming job of stripping and refinishing, take a few minutes to try out a cleaner-conditioner on one section to see what happens. It can do no harm and may save you a lot of unnecessary labor.

6-1. Cleaners and Conditioners

There are a lot of cleaners sold in supermarkets and hardware stores for reviving old finishes, but you can't do any better than a mixture of 3/4 boiled linseed oil and 1/4 turpentine. Properly applied, this conditioner will not only remove the dirt, but it will also disguise scratches, clean up haziness and restore the natural grain and color. It should be applied hot for badly soiled areas. There are a number of commercial products sold for the same purpose as this mix, and they are all fairly good, but try them out in a small, inconspicuous area before applying them to the whole surface.

If the cleanser-conditioner worked as magically as you hoped, you won't have to go any further. Just apply a coat of wax or two or some furniture polish to bring back the color.

Particularly bad areas such as grease spots can often be removed with simple "green soap", available at most drug stores. On the other hand, if the piece isn't in too bad condition and just looks a little dirty, you can use white soap and water. Be careful with water, though, since it can cause a whitish haze in shellac and lacquer (and the odds are heavy that one of these will be the finish on store-bought furniture). Even so, this condition, too, can be cured (see Section 6-5).

6-2. Types of Finishes You'll Find

At first, it seems impossibly difficult to determine what kind of finish was used on a

Fig. 6-1. A mixture of 3/4 boiled linseed oil and 1/4 turpentine makes an excellent cleaner-conditioner.

Fig. 6-2. To tell if a piece has been refinished in the past, inspect the carvings and the edges for traces of steel wool.

particular specimen. It isn't as difficult or mysterious as it may seem, however.

One myth that should be dispelled quickly is the furniture store pitch about the super varnish on whatever it is they're trying to sell you. True varnish finishes simply cannot be applied to mass-produced furniture. Any piece bought in a furniture store will undoubtedly have a lacquer finish – not a bad finish at that, but not varnish.

Furthermore, both varnish and lacquer are relatively recent inventions (around the turn of the century), so any piece that has been around a while is almost certainly finished with shellac; there is a good chance however that the piece has been refinished already – perhaps more than once.

After a while you'll be able to tell if a piece has been refinished or not just by looking at it. There are always telltale signs of scraping and sanding on a piece that has been refinished. Look at the carvings and the edges. Any traces of steel wool? Or look where there are chips or nicks in the finish. What's underneath? Another finish? Finally, look underneath to see if there are signs of two types of finishing materials. It may take a while to recognize these signs, but after you've gone through the process yourself a few times, the signposts will be unmistakably clear.

But even if you've found that the piece has been refinished a couple of times, does that help you to determine what finish was used? No, it doesn't (although the *lack* of a second finish on an old piece will tell you that the finish has to be shellac).

6-3. Testing for Finishes

The only sure way of determining which finish was used on a particular piece is through the use of chemicals.

Shellac – to test for shellac, wrap a piece of cloth around the end of your finger and dip it into some wood alcohol. Use the almost pure, denatured (poisonous) alcohol. Rubbing alcohol is no good since it is more than 3/4 water.

Fig. 6-3. To test for a varnish finish, apply varnish remover to an inconspicuous part of the piece of furniture.

Rub your finger across the surface of the piece. If the surface dissolves, you can be sure that it is shellac.

Lacquer – For lacquer dip the cloth in lacquer thinner. Lacquer will respond in a unique way to lacquer thinner. It will start to look worn or scuffed-up at that particular spot. Soon this look will disappear, as the highly volatile thinner evaporates, and the rubbed area will look glossy and smooth again (more so than before, usually).

Varnish – The only thing that can touch varnish is paint and varnish remover. Put a little bit of that on a spot where it doesn't matter much, then let it work. Paint remover will affect lacquer and shellac, too, however, so try their solvents first. There are exceptions to this test: *sometimes* lacquer thinner will react with *some* varnishes. But there is a difference. Lacquer thinner causes varnish to crinkle up, and it doesn't get smooth again after the thinner evaporates. Furthermore,

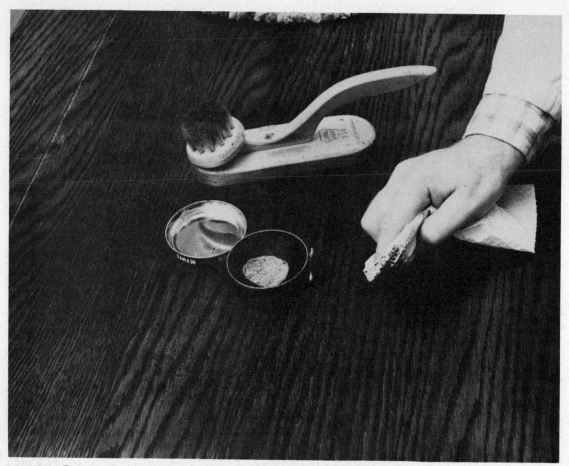

Fig. 6-4. Treat scuffed furniture with plain wax shoe polish.

varnish leaves the hardest surface, so try to dent any questionable surface with your fingernail. If it doesn't yield, you can be pretty sure it's varnish.

Other Finishes — There are other finishes, of course, paint being the most obvious. But there are also more exotic finishes like a combination of shellac and some primitive forms of lacquer. You may find this in pieces dating from around the time of the Civil War until after World War I. As far as cleaning is concerned, just treat these finishes as you would shellac. Special treatment is required, however, if you're trying to remove this finish (see Volume 16).

There are, of course, many other time-honored finishes applied by professional and amateur refinishers. Very rarely are these applied at the factory. Some of them are boiled linseed oil, clear sealer and French polish, none of which present any special problem in cleaning. They either wash off or have worn off spontaneously by the time you start fooling around with them. The only exception is wax, and wax may either be used alone even though it shouldn't be or over some other finish. If the piece has been around a while, you can be sure it got a couple of coats of wax at some time in its career.

6-4. Removing Wax

If you can see wax or suspect that a finish has a coat of wax, it must be removed before you can clean off the gook and grime. A can of

Fig. 6-5. It shellac or lacquer cracks, it may be repaired by a process called "reamalgamation".

Fig. 6-6.   *Before a piece can be stripped, it must be determined what finish it has.*

turpentine or mineral spirit and a little rubbing should remove most of the wax and leave the piece ready for cleaning.

6-5. White Spots and Rings

You usually find white spots and rings on shellac-finished tables, although they can occur with lacquer and less often with varnish. The culprit is usually a wet glass set down on the surface. Almost any fluid can damage the surface of unprotected shellac, however, which is a good reason for keeping such finishes well waxed.

If the white is more hazy than well-defined in a true ring or spot, you may get it out with the old refinisher's trick of rubbing a little cigar ash in with some saliva.

If that doesn't work, and it won't for anything other than the mildest cases, the next best bet is to polish the white area with a piece of fine (3/0) steel wool and a little oil. Any kind of light oil will do — lemon oil, mineral oil, corn oil, olive oil, sewing machine oil, linseed oil. As a matter of fact, almost any kind of non-water or non-alcoholic fluid, such as turpentine or mineral spirits, will do. Rub lightly for a long while.

This treatment should get off the majority of white spots, but if it doesn't, mix some common table salt into the oil. If *that* doesn't work, you'll have to resort to pumice, but be very careful not to rub too hard or too long. Mix the pumice into a paste, using water until it reaches a creamy consistency. Apply with oil as before. Use a padded sanding block, if you have one, to rub the spot with the pumice and oil mix; don't bear down too hard because the pumice may scratch the rest of the surface badly if you aren't careful.

If nothing else works, try a commercial product designed for this work. Whatever you use, wipe it off with a damp rag, let the surface dry, then follow with a healthy coat of furniture polish.

Somewhere along the line, before or after the polish coat, it may be apparent that the area you removed the spot from is going to stand out. In that case, you may have to apply the same treatment to the entire surface so that it all looks the same.

6-6. Scratches, Gouges and Other Wounds — Wax Sticks

Many shallow scratches can be removed from the finish by using a cleaner-conditioner as mentioned earlier. If that doesn't do it, a piece of the nut meat from the same source, (a walnut for walnut wood, etc.) rubbed diagonally across the crack a number of times should darken the scratch enough to make it fade away.

If the wood has been stained, you can try to match the stain with something similar. You can also try plain oil colors mixed to match the existing finish.

For deep scratches and gouges, some filling is necessary, and there are several products used for this.

The easiest materials to use are plain wax crayons which are melted over a sootless alcohol lamp and dripped into the wound. Most finish colors can be matched by one of those big crayon assortments that contains a lot of browns and reds. Mix these with some black, and white or yellow or both and you can arrive at a conglomeration that will duplicate anything.

The mixing itself is a little tricky. Shave off some wax chips, heat them and keep adding other colors until you get the shade you want. You have to heat up the mix every time and let it cool, because you can't tell whether it's orange or purple when it's hot. The wax cools rapidly, though, and shouldn't take too much time altogether.

When you get the mixture to just the shade you want, heat it up again and start dribbling it into the scratch. Scrape off the excess with a dull knife and level the scratch fill. Give the

Fig. 6-7. Shallow scratches can often be removed with a cleaner-conditioner.

top a stroke with your finger to make it smooth.

If the job looks good, it is wise to coat the entire surface with a coat of two parts alcohol and one part shellac. This prevents the wax from bleeding into varnish or lacquer. Then varnish the whole surface. You can, however, leave the scratch alone if it isn't on a surface where you'll be applying a new finish.

The new finish may contrast with the other surfaces, so either varnish the entire piece while you're at it, or rub the varnish coat with steel wool to give it the desired degree of dullness.

It should be noted here that you don't have to use crayons. There are special wax sticks, found in furniture shops and some hardware stores, which are made expressly for this purpose. Buy them if you prefer.

6-7. Deep Wounds — Stick Shellac

After wax, the other approved method is shellac sticks. These are preferred by the professionals and they do render a more invisible, professional look. They are not easy to use, however, and they cannot be removed easily if you louse up the job (wax can be pulled right out again). Our recommendation would be to use the wax for smaller, less conspicuous repairs, and use stick shellac for bad or obvious places. Shellac is available in many different shades, and you heat and combine if necessary. Use opaque for deep wounds and transparent for shallow ones.

To apply stick shellac, use your alcohol lamp to heat the blade of a knife. Also heat the end of the shellac stick and scrape off a little of the molten shellac and apply it into the hole. If the hole is deep, you should use several coats rather than filling it all at once.

After the hole is filled with the hot shellac, smooth it out with your hot knife, or — better — a flat spatula. Leave it slightly higher and rounded in the center of the patch if it is large.

When the shellac has cooled, cut it down level with the surface using a razor blade, sharp knife or the flat side of a chisel. Then finish the surface with some very fine wet or dry sandpaper and light oil.

Remember that nothing is going to stick — shellac or glue — if the area to be filled is very dirty or soiled. Clean it thoroughly; if you're going to stain, do so before applying the patch. You can patch edges and corners also with stick shellac if you make forms out of tongue depressors and masking tape, filling the area so formed.

Stick lacquer is also available and is used in the same manner as stick shellac. Another material you can use is wood dough, but this doesn't give a very good finish. The best usage for this is in inconspicuous places, or as a filler in deep wounds over which stick wax or shellac is applied.

6-8. Cigarette Burns

For a burn that is not too deep or extensive, treat like any other wound in the surface — with wax or shellac sticks. Here, though, you should dig out the burned materials and leave a clean hole. Use a razor blade to dress the wound.

When the burn is deep, the entire surface may need refinishing. With solid wood, first sand down the surface to bare, unburned material, then stain and finish as outlined in Chapters 1 and 2 of Volume 16. If the top is veneer, and the burn goes through the veneer, patch the veneer as described later in this chapter, then refinish (see Chapter 2, Volume 16).

6-9. Dents and Bruises

A little dent in the surface of an antique can be passed off as an authenticating feature, but it can be merely an eyesore in most pieces. Dents and bruises can be removed from all but the hardest woods (hard-rock maple, for example).

Wood fibers act in much the same way as the pores of sponges. If you fill them with moisture they will swell and warp. Look at your doors and windows in humid weather. Warping is an advantage when it comes to dents, however, for it is the moisture absorption of the fibers that eliminates the dent.

There are several ways to utilize the moisture absorption principle. One is to put some water in the depression and watch it swell, but this doesn't work very well on most hardwoods. The best general solution for any dent is to steam the dent up to level with a regular household iron and a wet cloth. Lay the cloth over the dent with the iron on top. Turn the iron onto a low or "synthetic" setting and let it work for a half hour or more. Keep half an eye on it while you go about other chores, so that it doesn't swell up too high; the chances are, however, that the dent will not rise enough rather than rise too high.

If simple steaming doesn't work, you can try sticking a needle into the depression, making some tiny holes for better absorption, then proceeding as above. The swelling will either close up the holes or render them too small to notice. Give the needle a little whack with the hammer to make it penetrate the surface. A quarter-inch or so is deep enough.

All that water won't help the finish any, so you may as well remove it from the area before you begin. This will help the absorption process. When you're done, refinish as described in Chapter 2 of Volume 16. You might get away with just redoing the area you worked on, but chances are you'll wind up finishing the whole surface.

Be careful, by the way, with old pieces and dents near glue lines. All that heat and steam may loosen up the joints. For such cases, put a piece of wet blotter into the depression, press a marble or similar rounded object over it, and hold the iron on top of that. Turn the iron on a little hotter (medium range or higher) since it is so far from the wood. No matter how you do it, try to keep the water and steam away from the glued areas.

Very hard woods, as mentioned above, will not succumb to steam, but then again, they are very hard to bruise. If it does happen, the fibers are probably broken rather than compressed. You will either have to sand the surrounding surfaces to minimize the abruptness of the dent, or fill the area with a shellac or wax stick as described earlier in this chapter.

6-10. Cloudiness, Haziness, Blushing

"Cloudiness", "haziness" and "blushing" refer to the same phenomenon. As a matter of fact, cloudiness, hazing or blushing is nothing more than a large white ring or spot and should be treated accordingly (see Section 6-5).

What causes the condition is some sort of moisture getting into the finish either through excess humidity in the air or a lack of heat in the room. The water that collects on the surface causes the same problem over the entire surface as that spilled martini did to the cocktail table top.

If the finish is cracked or "alligatored" in addition to being cloudy, refer to the following section. "Reamalgamation", as the corrective process is called, will fix up clouding in addition to alligatoring.

6-11. Cracking, Crazing, Alligatoring

Furniture that is directly in the path of hot sunlight or is left for long periods in a hot attic will often develop a condition known by such various names as "cracking", "crazing", "crawling" or "alligatoring". Technically, the terms have somewhat different meanings. A *crawl* is a large *craze*, for example. The condition is often accompanied by clouding or hazing as well. Regardless of the size or

Fig. 6-8.   *Once revived through refinishing, furniture acquires a beauty it may not have had originally.*

pattern of the cracks, the cure is happily much simpler than the explanation of the terms.

As mentioned above, finishing material is usually either shellac or lacquer, both of which can be dissolved and spread around again without removal. The technique is known as "reamalgamation" and is accomplished by applying a solvent to the finish with a rag or brush. The solvent "melts" the finish enough so that it can be redistributed or reworked over the entire surface.

The first step is to find out what the finish is (see Section 6-3). When that is settled, use denatured alcohol to reamalgamate shellac and lacquer thinner for lacquer. If you run into one of those intermediate early 20th century finishes, use three parts of alcohol to one part lacquer thinner. That should cover all the bases except for varnish (see Section 6-13 for the solution for cracked varnish).

6-12. Reamalgamation Technique

The process of reamalgamation is the same regardless of the solvent used. First, remove all traces of wax as described in Section 6-4. Next, apply the solvent with a clean brush. It must be very clean. Buy a new brush if you have any doubt, a lacquer brush for lacquer or a shellac brush for shellac. About two or two-and-a-half inches is the best size. It's a good idea to experiment in an inconspicuous spot before attempting a large surface.

You should make sure to have a level surface when applying the solvent, at least over large areas. It is also best to apply the solvent in long, wide, even strokes across the grain and then brush again with the grain. This will often be enough for minor cracking, but if it isn't, keep repeating the process until the cracks are gone.

The one thing you'll have to watch for if you keep adding more and more solvent (it's very volatile and evaporates rapidly), is that you don't cut too deep with it. The key point is when the surface is free of all cracks but still has a few brush marks or mild blemishes. Try

stopping there and waiting until the surface dries. In a way, what you're doing is applying a new coat of the finish and you don't expect a perfect look until it dries, so don't expect it here. Afterwards, if it still looks bad, give it another go. But it should dry up looking nice.

Once you're satisfied with the general look, it may be well to give the surface another coat. This is more desirable with shellac than lacquer, but it won't hurt a lacquer finish either. After that's applied, give the surface a rubdown with fine 3/0 steel wool and a coat of wax or polish. Then step back and admire your handiwork.

It may be well to read the respective descriptions on how to apply lacquer or shellac in Chapter 2, Volume 16, since reamalgamation requires similar techniques. One thing about shellac, in particular, should be considered — do not apply it in damp weather.

6-13. Cracked, Chipped Varnish

Varnish will sometimes crack, although not half as easily as lacquer and shellac. Often it becomes chipped, too, and the cures for both are essentially the same. Unfortunately, varnish revamping is a much more difficult and chancy proposition than reamalgamation. You'll have to buy some special chemicals called "amalgamatons", which are sold at larger paint and hardware stores. They are sold under various trade names, but mainly contain acetone and other harsh ingredients. Watch out for these chemicals; try them out in an out-of-the-way place to see if they will work for you.

You can always try another method, which is also used for chipped varnish surfaces. Buy one of the modern synthetic varnishes and work it into the cracks or chipped areas, applying a second, third or fourth coat until the depressions are completely filled. Then paint over the entire area with a final coat.

As you have probably determined for

yourself, you may be better off removing the entire finish and starting over.

6-14. Black Rings or Spots

It would seem that this problem would be similar to "white spots", but there is a difference: white spots are nearly always superficial and easy to eradicate; black spots are almost always caused by water that has penetrated the finish and gotten right into the wood itself. This condition is frequently caused by water condensing on a flower vase. The fact that the vase remains in one place for days at a time is the reason that the moisture penetrates so deeply. Shellac can be penetrated in a day, varnish in a week or two.

No matter what the cause, the cure lies in first removing the finish from the entire surface. This is really the only way to get at the bare wood. The black spot is bleached out rather easily with oxalic acid, which may be bought in crystal form then dissolved in water. Oxalic acid won't hurt your hands unless you have a cut or scratch, in which case you should wear rubber gloves. If the acid scares

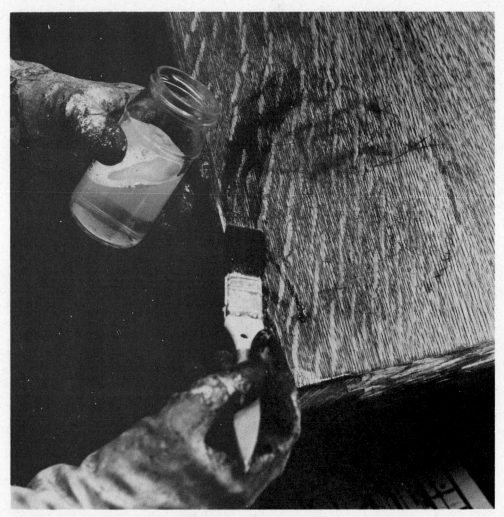

Fig. 6-9. Black rings are almost always caused by water that has penetrated the finish and gotten into the wood itself.

you, regular household ammonia works almost as well.

All you have to do is rub the oxalic acid over the spot and it should disappear; there is a problem, however, if the wood has been given a coat of stain (which it probably has). The stain, too, will come out, so you may as well treat the entire surface with the acid so that it will look the same all over. The oxalic acid will leave tiny crystals on the surface, so wash it with vinegar before refinishing. Restain, too, if desired, before refinishing.

6-15. Scuffed Finishes

Use plain wax shoe polish for scuffed furniture. The shoe polish will not only bring some color back to the wood, but fill all those gouges and imperfections as well. To do the best job, precede the wax treatment with a coat or two of colored polish (dyes in mineral oil). Follow afterwards with a coat of plain paste wax over the entire surface.

6-16. Grease Spots

Surface grease is no problem: it is easily removed with soap, detergent or cleaner-conditioner, as described in the beginning of this chapter. Occasionally, however, the grease penetrates to the bare wood, mainly because of a thin or crumbling finish.

Deep grease spots which have penetrated into the wood can be eliminated by using a dry cleaning fluid like those used for clothes. Benzine, ''Energine'', or similar products should get rid of most animal stains. Acetone is better for vegetable oils. Use a small brush and try not to let the cleaner get onto areas other than the stain. Apply liberally until the grease spot is gone, wiping dry with tissue paper after each application.

6-17. Chipped or Peeling Paint

Painted furniture has either an opaque lacquer or enamel finish. If this has peeled, there really isn't anything to do except strip it and repaint (or use another finish if the wood looks okay). One expert suggests trying to glue down a large ''peel'' as long as it is flexible and smooth, but this isn't a very satisfactory cure. Whatever caused the peeling (moisture probably) is still there underneath, and there seems little doubt that you'll wind up stripping the whole thing anyway.

Chipping can be masked, if not exactly cured.

The first step is to find out whether the finish is enamel or lacquer. Lacquer thinner will cause the usual reaction to lacquer, and won't affect enamel at all. If you have a lacquer surface, reamalgamation (see Section 6-12) should do the trick. Enamel is a little more difficult. You have to find a matching color and apply several thin layers until the chipped area is brought up level with the surrounding area. Feather the chipped edges before starting, and sand with 6/0 sandpape between coats. Allow 24 hours between layers.

If a lacquer chip is very large, reamalgamation won't work. You'll have to apply new lacquer, using the same method as with enamel. No doubt your new surface is going to look a lot shinier than the old one, so try to dull the spot by buffing with 3/0 steel wool.

6-18. Milk Paint

In case you have an old-fashioned milk-paint finish, you should consider yourself lucky because it will be considered valuable by antique experts. If ordinary cleaning won't make the finish look any better, leave it alone. These finishes have a certain charm, even when sort of ugly.

You can even fix milk paints, but it's a tricky job at best. The old-timers used sour milk mixed up with whatever happened to be around. Black, for instance, was made from soot out of kerosene lamps; brown and other earth colors were literally that — various forms of clay, loam, and sand. Red was made from blood, blue from blueberry juice.

6-19. Repairing Veneer and Inlays

Wood veneers are usually the most beautiful part of furniture. When something happens to them, the piece takes on a seedy look. Fortunately, they are great subjects for worthwhile restoration because veneer is not difficult to fix and the piece will look amazingly better once the job is done.

Loose or blistered veneer can often be reglued as is by warming up and melting the old glue (probably fish hide) with a clothes iron. Cover the area with wax paper and thin padding. Slit any large blisters along the grain with a razor blade if you can't get under them. When the blisters do go down, there will probably be an overlap at the slit, because the wood has undoubtedly been swollen. Use a new razor blade and pare off that part of the veneer that overlapped (have a steady eye and hand).

If the veneer is loose at the edges and dirt has gotten inside, the best thing to do is break that piece off and scrape off the old dirt and glue. Hopefully, the break will occur at a natural point and not be noticeable when it is reglued. You can always fill any large cracks with stick wax or shellac, but it shouldn't be necessary.

Inlays are nothing more than strips or bits of veneer and should be treated accordingly. Since they are small, you can often lift them out completely, scrape off all the old glue and grime, then glue them on again.

Missing veneer or inlay material is a bad business, but maybe not as hopeless as it appears. It should be possible to match the old veneer somewhere (after all, there aren't that many types of woods). Maybe you won't find an exact match, color-for-color or grain-for-grain, but you should be able to find a piece that will do. If it's a small inlay, perhaps you can take out all the pieces that match and put in a whole new series or section that is completely different but looks okay because it isn't an obvious mismatch. We much prefer replacing entire sections of veneer to patching (see below).

Where do you find new materials? If you've been refinishing for some time and listening to the old-timers' advice about saving good veneer, you may find a piece right in your workshop. Failing that, a local cabinetmaker may have a matching piece, or you may be able to find a similar piece and steal from that.

6-20. Patches

Many authorities on furniture repair tell you how to make patches for badly damaged surfaces. Patching a piece in the middle strikes us as futile. If the piece *is* worth the aggravation, then take it to a pro. Patching is a delicate art which you can attempt on a relatively worthless piece if you enjoy the work. But if the piece is any good, take it to somebody who knows what he's doing.

For the record, though, here's how it's done for a solid surface:

- Find a piece of seasoned wood which will approximate the piece in color and grain. Wood from an old piece is best, but be sure to thoroughly remove all finishing materials and dirt. Lay it over the area to be matched to find the best grain match.

- Cut the piece in the shape of a diamond, arrow, parallelogram or anything but a square or rectangle. For some reason, 90° angles show up too easily. Sand thoroughly.

- Lay the new piece over the surface to be

Fig. 6-10. This old chair has had one of its spindles replaced.

patched and delicately scribe around the perimeter. If the patch is so deep it distorts the shape, make a template of the top and transcribe.

- Dig a "grave", using the scribed perimeter.

The grave should have vertical edges and a level bottom to match the cut piece as exactly as possible.

- Try the patch in the grave and trim, cut or sand any inaccuracies.

Fig. 6-11. Types of hardware.

- When the patch fits perfectly, lay it in with casein glue to fill the cavities. The patch may extend slightly above the surface and be sanded or cut down to level.

Veneer can be patched in the same way if desired, except that the grave is only as deep as the veneer. If you must patch inlays or veneer, find a place where the old veneer was

Fig. 6-12. Brass hardware is best cleaned with commercial brass cleaner.

matched or the grain ends naturally, and replace the entire section. You've got to be a good cabinetmaker to put a patch in veneer and make it look decent.

6-21. Hardware Restoration

If you have original brass drawer pulls, keyhole plates, hinges or escutcheons, don't discard them just because they're tarnished. Solid brass can be cleaned with ammonia or a commercial brass cleaner. Stubborn areas can be scrubbed with lemon rind or hot vinegar and table salt. Remove the hardware if it's easier and dip it into a cleaning agent. Rub the cleaned surfaces with 3/0 steel wool, then clean with warm, soapy water, rinse and dry to give the hardware just the right look.

Brass-plated hardware is best cleaned with commercial brass cleaner or rottenstone and boiled linseed oil in a thin paste. Wipe off the paste with more linseed oil, then polish. Wash with warm, soapy water as above.

If the hardware is ruined beyond repair or missing, you're probably better off replacing everything than trying to match what you have, especially if it comes in pairs.

6-22. Plastic

A lot of new furniture is made out of plastic, both hard and soft. The hard laminates, often referred to by one of the brand names, "Formica", are best protected by a silicone-base wax. The wax helps prevent wear and makes cleaning easier. Soft plastic, usually vinyl, can be protected by one of the vinyl preservatives sold commercially. Those used for car tops are as good as any.

When a hard plastic surface becomes worn or dull, pour a little cleaner-polisher on the worn area and rub with a soft cloth pad in the long direction. Rub until the gloss reappears, then wipe dry. Apply a coat of wax to the entire surface. Never use abrasive cleaners on laminated plastic.

When laminated plastic comes loose from its wood backing, it can be replaced by scraping off the old adhesive and gluing it back into place again with a counter top adhesive. Clamp down until the adhesive dries.

6-23. Leather

Leather has been around almost as long as wood, although it usually doesn't last as long. It can be revived, however, if it hasn't cracked or otherwise deteriorated. To bring back the old glow and also to preserve it, occasionally rub it down with saddle soap or castile soap. Don't use regular furniture polish or anything similar, since these materials contain harmful solvents.

To clean dirty leather, mix up some mild soap flakes (not detergent) with warm water and a teaspoon of vinegar. Apply to the leather with a soft, clean rag and wash off with clear lukewarm water. Finish, when dry, with a little leather dressing. All these materials can be obtained from a saddle shop or leather shop. Sometimes shoe repair stores carry the same or similar materials.

6-24. Marble Tops

Marble is basically limestone. Since it is porous, it is rather easily scratched and stained below the surface. If ordinary cleaning won't remove dirty marks, then the mark is a deep stain.

The only way to restore a damaged marble surface is by literally grinding it down. This is done in stages, using various grit-abrasive papers and some sort of powder such as rottenstone or tin oxide (available at most drugstores). Start with a very fine grit such as 10/0 to see how deep the scratch or stain is. Some may come off with just one treatment. If this does nothing, skip to a 3/0 or even 1/0 grit for severely damaged surfaces; keep rubbing evenly across the surface, using finer and finer grits until the finish is like new.

If there are professional marble finishers in your area (try the yellow pages — you'll be surprised), it's best to take advantage of their professional skills. Marble-topped pieces can be quite valuable, so whatever you spend is probably worth it.